The Consumption of Wealth

The Consumption of Wealth

Master Consumption of Wealth Economics for Social Progress and Sustainable Prosperity Today

(Illustrated, Refined & Edited)

Simon N. Patten

Copyright Notice for Readers

Publication Year: 2026
Publisher: DD Books
ISBN: 9789372449181

Edition: First Edition, 2026
Contact: ddsalesglobal@gmail.com

Book: The Consumption of Wealth
Author: Simon N. Patten
Price: Rs 250/-

Table of Content

Reader Note

Simon N. Patten's *The Consumption of Wealth* is not merely an economic treatise; it is a profound reflection on how human desire, comfort, and progress shape civilization itself. Long before consumer psychology became a recognized discipline, Patten explored the emotional and social dimensions of consumption—the way we attach feeling to food, goods, land, and home, and how these attachments drive both personal happiness and national growth. For modern readers, this book remains startlingly relevant in an age defined by excess, sustainability challenges, and questions about what true wealth really means.

In Chapter 1, "The Causes of the Intensity of Feeling Derived from Food," Patten delves into one of humanity's most primal yet complex pleasures—the sensory and psychological satisfaction derived from eating. He connects the act of consumption to emotion, community, and memory, suggesting that food is not only nourishment but also one of the earliest expressions of wealth and civilization.

Chapter 2 examines how the cost of commodities influences their consumption, revealing that value is not simply economic but psychological. Cheapness can dull appreciation, while scarcity intensifies desire—a timeless observation that echoes in today's debates about fast fashion, overconsumption, and luxury culture.

Moving deeper, Chapter 3 exposes the causes that obscure the true laws of consumption, pointing to habit, imitation, and cultural conditioning as forces that cloud rational decision-making. In this, Patten anticipates modern behavioral economics, showing how emotion often outpaces reason in shaping demand.

As readers journey into Chapter 4, "The Growth of New Pleasures," they encounter a fascinating analysis of how societies evolve through expanding desires.

Each new age invents fresh forms of happiness—art, technology, entertainment—and yet these innovations often create both liberation and dependency.

The later chapters—"The Love of Home and Country," "The Standard of Life," and "The Best Use of Land"—move beyond materialism to explore moral and civic wealth. Patten believed that prosperity was not measured by possession but by how wisely resources were used to foster stability, unity, and aesthetic satisfaction.

His reflections on the standard of life prefigure modern discussions about sustainability, wellbeing, and ethical economics.

Finally, in "The Outlook for the Future," Patten's vision stretches forward—a hopeful yet cautionary meditation on humanity's ability to align comfort with conscience, pleasure with prudence, and growth with gratitude.

Readers who open this volume will find not a dry economic argument but an intellectual journey through the psychology of satisfaction, the ethics of wealth, and the future of civilization itself. Patten's insight, expressed with clarity and conviction, urges us to reconsider not just what we consume, but *why* we consume—and whether our habits are building a richer life or merely filling an emptier one.

This book rewards both the reflective reader and the critical thinker. It offers an enduring intellectual delight—a chance to reexamine the modern world's obsession with wealth through the eyes of a man who understood that true prosperity lies not in possession but in the wise enjoyment of what sustains life and elevates the human spirit.

Publisher's Note

When *The Consumption of Wealth* by Simon N. Patten first appeared, it emerged as a pioneering text that challenged the purely production-centered focus of classical economics. Patten redirected the reader's attention toward the often-neglected realm of consumption, arguing that how societies use their wealth is just as vital as how they create it.

In this modern edition, we have sought to preserve the author's original analytical depth while refining the language and structure for contemporary readability—allowing twenty-first-century readers to experience Patten's brilliance without the barrier of antiquated phrasing.

Patten was a scholar of exceptional foresight. Long before the terms *consumer behavior* or *standard of living* became academic commonplaces, he explored their ethical and psychological foundations. His reflections on the interplay between pleasure and cost, habit and innovation, luxury and morality form the conceptual groundwork for much of what we now call behavioral economics.

The chapters of this book move progressively from the individual to the collective, from appetite to aspiration—from the enjoyment of food and comfort to the moral structure of nations. This edition aims to bring Patten's ideas to life for a generation that faces its own crises of consumption: environmental depletion, consumer fatigue, and the search for meaning in an age of abundance. His observations on "the intensity of feeling derived from food" and "the influence of cost upon consumption" feel almost prophetic in a world shaped by advertising, social media, and global capitalism.

Similarly, his discussions of "the love of home and country" and "the best use of land" remind us that wealth's truest test lies in the health of communities and the stewardship of the Earth.

Our editorial approach has been guided by two principles: fidelity to Patten's intellectual integrity, and clarity for the modern reader.

The original tone of earnest inquiry and moral engagement has been carefully maintained, while archaic expressions have been gently clarified to preserve fluency without diminishing authenticity.

We believe that readers should encounter Patten not as a relic of nineteenth-century economics, but as a voice of enduring relevance—one that speaks to the ethical tensions of contemporary life with striking modernity.

In reissuing this classic, the publisher seeks to honor Patten's conviction that economics must be a moral science—that wealth, to have meaning, must be directed toward the enrichment of human life.

His words challenge us to question our own assumptions: What is the purpose of comfort? What is the moral dimension of pleasure? Can consumption ever be wise, beautiful, or just?

We invite readers, scholars, and seekers alike to explore these pages not merely as a study of economic forces but as a meditation on the very art of living well.

The Consumption of Wealth remains a timeless guide to understanding the delicate balance between material gain and spiritual fulfillment—a balance every age must rediscover for itself.

Introduction

Simon N. Patten's The Consumption of Wealth stands at the intersection of economics, psychology, and moral philosophy—a work that dares to ask not how wealth is earned, but how it is experienced. While most economists of his time celebrated production as the engine of progress, Patten looked beyond factories and finance to the inner world of the human being—the desires, satisfactions, and values that give wealth its meaning. This book begins not with the market, but with the senses. In its opening chapter, Patten explores the deep emotional resonance of food—how flavor, memory, and culture intertwine to transform necessity into delight. From that simple act of eating, he constructs a far-reaching theory of consumption that explains the evolution of pleasure, the shaping of habits, and the soul of prosperity itself.

As the chapters unfold, Patten's vision broadens. He examines how cost influences desire, how comfort breeds both stability and complacency, and how societies constantly redefine pleasure in the face of changing technology and environment. His analysis of the "growth of new pleasures" remains eerily relevant: from the birth of industrial luxuries to today's digital distractions, human happiness is ever caught between innovation and exhaustion.

Yet beneath his intellectual rigor runs a strong current of humanism. In The Love of Home and Country, Patten reveals that true wealth resides not in material accumulation but in emotional attachment—to place, to family, to shared ideals. His discussion of The Standard of Life reframes economic progress as a question of dignity and moral aspiration rather than consumption alone.

Perhaps the book's greatest achievement is its prophetic scope. In The Best Use of Land and The Outlook for the Future, Patten speaks to ecological balance and the ethical use of resources long before such concerns became mainstream. His call for "rational enjoyment" anticipates today's movements toward sustainability, mindful consumption, and the redefinition of prosperity in human—not merely financial—terms. Modern readers will find in these pages a rare combination of intellectual depth and personal resonance. Patten writes with the precision of an economist, the curiosity of a psychologist, and the moral conviction of a philosopher. His insights pierce through centuries to confront our present dilemmas: why are we never satisfied, even in abundance? How can pleasure become creative rather than destructive? What does it mean to live richly, not merely to live well?

The Consumption of Wealth is, ultimately, a journey of rediscovery. It invites readers to trace the moral evolution of desire—from hunger to art, from comfort to culture, from possession to peace. To read it today is to confront both our heritage and our future—to realize that every act of consumption is also an act of self-definition.

Simon N. Patten gives us not a manual of economics, but a philosophy of living—a reminder that the worth of wealth lies not in what it buys, but in what it inspires. His work endures as a mirror for every generation seeking to reconcile progress with purpose and pleasure with principle.

Chapter-1
The Causes of the Intensity of Feeling Derived from Food

Why does food move us so deeply—sometimes beyond mere hunger? This chapter uncovers how human appetite was shaped not by comfort, but by survival, scarcity, and struggle. Tracing the journey from primitive feasting to modern satiety, it reveals why our pleasures, cravings, and limits around food are not fixed instincts, but evolving responses to history, labor, environment, and abundance.

It is impossible to precisely determine the laws that govern the strength of sensations and feelings we derive from eating food without examining the past development of human beings. If humanity had always enjoyed an abundance and variety of food like that available to the more advanced societies today, there might be some justification for assuming that our current appetites are the result of some unchanging element in human nature. However, this is far from the case. Only a few generations ago, our ancestors lived in completely different circumstances—circumstances in which a sharp appetite was their main source of pleasure. Only those who had a strong craving for food could endure the hardships they faced and be motivated enough to work under conditions where the rewards of labor were minimal.

Primitive humans had no steady means of livelihood. With no certainty about the future, they had to take whatever food they could find, whenever and wherever nature chose to provide it. At certain times of the year, fish were plentiful; at others, game was abundant; and in yet other seasons, fruits or grains offered a temporary means of survival. But no matter how plentiful these resources might be at specific times, they were followed by long periods when food became extremely scarce. During such lean times, hunger and famine took a heavy toll, eliminating all those who lacked the physical strength and endurance to survive on very little. Thus, cycles of plenty and starvation followed each other in quick succession. One month, people would feast on nature's abundant offerings; the next, they would be near starvation, living only on what reserves their bodies had built up during the period of abundance in the form of muscle and fat.

One conclusion about such people can be stated with confidence: their appetite for food had to be exceptionally strong. If their hunger had been weak, they would have eaten just enough to satisfy their immediate needs during good times. When the season of scarcity arrived, their bodies would have been too frail to handle the harsh conditions, and they would have succumbed to illness or famine. Such a person had to have the ability to store fat in the body, just like a pig or a cow. And to achieve this, he needed to have an intense desire for food—an appetite so strong that he would continue eating long after his current bodily needs had already been met.

The powerful appetite of primitive humans is clearly visible in their behavior. When they had food, they showed no understanding of moderation. If they managed to kill an animal, they would immediately prepare a massive feast, devouring in a single day enough food to have sustained them for an entire week.

These people seemed to have no limit to their hunger and would only stop eating when they could physically eat no more. This overwhelming craving for food was evident in many other behaviors as well. The many revolting dishes they enjoyed with visible pleasure demonstrate just how overpowering this drive to consume was. Surely, no one not ruled by an extreme appetite would find pleasure in eating half-rotten meat, which many tribes considered a delicacy.

The early human being needed such a strong appetite to survive the brutal conditions created by an unpredictable food supply. A weaker appetite would have left them ill-suited to their environment and eventually led to their extinction. Over time, however, the gradual but consistent progress of human society led to more stable food sources. As starvation and famine became less frequent, a major transformation occurred. Eventually, among the more civilized societies of today, the availability of food has become so reliable that the average person rarely, if ever, experiences the true pain of hunger.

No one, I trust, will disagree that as the supply of food has become more consistent and reliable, the strength of human appetite has declined. The craving for heavy, coarse food in large quantities has almost entirely vanished. Feasting no longer takes the form of prolonged, gluttonous indulgences that stretch on for several days. Certainly, we are still far from reaching a perfect balance between our appetites and the modern conditions in which we live, but we have at least advanced to the point where the rough foods and harsh drinks that pleased our ancestors are now repulsive to us.

We must therefore examine what changes occur when a population that has relied on a single type of food begins to shift to a more diverse diet. This shift often comes through changes that equalize the cost of producing several essential kinds of food. Let us take, for example, a man whose diet consists entirely of potatoes. At his meal, the first potato he eats will give him a great deal of pleasure. He will also enjoy the second, though his appetite will already be less sharp. With each additional potato, the pleasure he receives diminishes, until finally, he reaches a point where no more enjoyment can be had from eating. This is known as the "point of satiety," and the location of this point greatly influences a person's habits and character. Will the appetite be satisfied after three potatoes? Or will it take four—or even more? Clearly, there is a link between this point of satiety and what the body physically needs.

A person who uses his brain more than his muscles will usually feel satisfied much sooner while eating than someone who does heavy manual labor. Modern machinery has taken over much of the difficult physical work that once required great strength, allowing people today to live with smaller appetites than in the past. It is also evident that people who spend their days indoors and work at sedentary jobs gradually lose part of their appetite. For them, food no longer offers as much pleasure as it once did when they were more active and exposed to fresh air and movement. Such facts are easily observable in everyday life by anyone paying attention. They show that the desire for food is not a fixed quantity—it changes with one's surroundings. As important as these observations are, however, they should not be treated as more significant than the transformations in appetite caused by the growing regularity of the food supply.

Yet, changes like these often go unnoticed, simply because they cannot be observed directly. It is only through a careful study of history that the major shifts in taste and appetite become visible. People tend to assume that the primitive man was essentially the same as the modern man. They often lack the kind of training necessary to grasp a vivid understanding of human development over time. Moreover, the idea that human nature is unchanging has long been reinforced by our philosophical traditions. Many basic economic assumptions are rooted in these philosophical beliefs, and it becomes difficult to break free from them and replace them with ideas that reflect the slow, steady development that history actually reveals.

There is yet another important result of human progress that deserves attention in this context. Primitive humans had very little shelter. The warmth of their bodies came from the large quantities of food they consumed, not from artificial sources like houses or clothing. Their protection against cold came from their own blood, rather than from the kind of buildings and garments that now protect nearly everyone.

It is only in recent times that homes and public buildings have been constructed well enough to provide full protection from outside weather. Even today, in many parts of the civilized world, fire is still used sparingly to heat homes, churches, and other buildings. Many people alive today can still remember a time when churches in this country were not heated. Anyone who has traveled in Europe can attest to how limited the use of indoor heating is in churches and even private residences. Similarly, the steadily increasing amount of clothing sold to all civilized nations reflects the growing dependence on artificial protection from cold and dampness.

These developments have reduced the body's need for food, and as a result, the appetite must also decrease until it aligns with what the body actually requires.

The point at which satiety is reached is further influenced by the nutritional value of the food being consumed. Certain types of food contain a higher proportion of nutrients, and thus, a smaller amount of these foods is sufficient to meet the body's needs compared to less nutritious options.

For example, if a person accustomed to a meat-based diet were forced to live on potatoes alone, his appetite would diminish long before he had consumed enough to meet his nutritional requirements. Conversely, if someone used to a potato-based diet suddenly began eating meat, his appetite would be so strong that he would consume far more meat than his body actually required.

Suppose a man whose only food has been potatoes now finds himself in a situation where wheat bread becomes a substantial part of his meals. Clearly, his appetite would be too strong for the new conditions.

If he eats half his usual portion of potatoes and then switches to bread, he will end up eating more bread than would be nutritionally equivalent to the remaining potatoes he would have otherwise eaten.

The introduction of a new food revives the appetite, and the person tends to eat more than the body needs. At the same time, when the diet becomes more varied, the body's need for food is actually reduced. Different kinds of food complement one another, and the body's full range of requirements can be met with less overall intake and less waste than with a single-type diet. If, then, a person's appetite grows as the variety of food increases—while at the same time the body's need for food decreases with a more balanced diet—then the shift toward a varied diet disrupts the earlier harmony between bodily needs and the appetite.

This harmony can only be restored when the appetite is moderated enough that the point of satiety is reached precisely when the system's nutritional needs are met. As the variety of our food increases, the intensity of pleasure we derive from eating must naturally diminish, so that once the body adjusts to the new diet, the point of satiety will be reached more quickly than before.

In real life, the truth of this law is often obscured by the particular conditions under which our civilizations have developed. In most societies during their early stages, the most enjoyable foods could not be consumed in large quantities because they were too expensive. In contrast, cheaper items like potatoes and rice were widely consumed, even though the pleasure they provided was far less than that of tastier, costlier foods. Today, however, a more varied diet typically includes a larger share of these more desirable items—such as wheat bread, meat, and alcoholic beverages. As a result, a varied diet stimulates the appetite in two ways: through its diversity and its tastiness, both of which increase the pleasure we associate with eating. Over time, however, the human appetite will gradually adjust to these new conditions, and the enjoyment derived from food will decrease until the point of satiety aligns once again with the body's actual needs.

There is no necessary relationship between the pleasure we feel from eating and the food's ability to nourish our bodies. Water and air are essential for life, yet we experience very little pleasure in consuming them. An abundant supply of any food quickly causes us to lose our taste for it. This is clearly seen in the way increased liquor consumption affects the preferences of drinkers. It is widely recognized that the demand for strong alcoholic drinks is rapidly growing.

Even in countries like France and Germany, where lighter drinks have traditionally been popular, the public's taste has become less refined than it once was. The shift from light to strong drinks indicates that people are losing the fine sensitivity that once brought intense pleasure from flavor and are now trying to replace that experience by consuming more and turning to stronger stimulation.

This decrease in appetite is also reflected in the growing variety of drinks people consume. Individuals with strong appetites typically have one favorite drink and often look down on others who prefer something different. But when people begin drinking multiple kinds of liquor in succession, it suggests a weakening of the appetite—because with a weaker appetite, the point of satiety for one kind of drink is reached long before the overall craving for alcohol has been satisfied.

With tobacco as well, we can observe the effects of a declining appetite. The abandonment of snuffing and chewing shows that these coarser forms of tobacco use have become distasteful—something that would not have happened if the strength of the appetite had remained as it once was. The growing use of stronger tobacco for smoking reflects the same change that we see in the increasing popularity of strong alcoholic drinks.

Today, most tobacco no longer comes from places like Cuba—renowned for the fine flavor of their product—but rather from areas like Wisconsin or Connecticut, which grow coarser tobacco. The rise in cigarette use further illustrates this trend, as even the stems of tobacco leaves can now be smoked in this form. However, I do not intend to suggest that every increase in food variety automatically reduces the pleasure we derive from eating. The initial enjoyment of the first portions of each food item may still be just as intense as ever, and yet, the feeling of satiety for that item is reached much sooner than it would be if that one food made up the entire meal. In refined individuals, the pleasure from the first few bites may be slightly reduced, but the most significant change lies in how quickly satiety is reached.

A small portion brings delight, but a large quantity becomes unappealing. By contrast, for their ancestors, abundance itself was part of the pleasure. They could eat an entire meal consisting of just one item and find it enjoyable all the way through.

A person has a strong appetite if they do not reach the point of satiety with a single item until the stomach is completely full. Someone who can make an entire meal out of soup is a clear example. A diet consisting of salt pork and potatoes also indicates a strong appetite. The preference for fatty meats, especially those cooked in grease, tells the same story. Likewise, a love for the traditional boiled dinner—where everything is cooked together so that all ingredients take on the same flavor—comes from the same cause

In general, the stronger the appetite, the fewer the types of food needed to satisfy it. Other options are rejected because the continued pleasure from the familiar food remains stronger than the appeal of anything else. In someone with a strong appetite, a long and complete satisfaction of a single craving is followed by a sleepy or sluggish state, lasting until hunger reawakens the desire. The boa constrictor is an extreme example of this kind of appetite, remaining mostly inactive unless driven by hunger.

A person with a weak appetite may still be perfectly healthy, but they reach the point of satiety for any one item so quickly that they must eat several different foods to meet their nutritional needs. Such a person constantly shifts from one dish to another while eating, trying to keep their appetite stimulated by the taste of something new. Just a few bites of any dish are enough to satisfy them, and the desire for that item does not return until it is reawakened by sampling something else. The urge to sip a drink continually while eating arises from the same cause.

A fresh, cool, or especially hot drink offers a sudden change in sensation, which revives the appetite. In this way, the appetite gains a renewed vigor from the contrast in experience. Having a weak appetite means one enjoys individual sensations more intensely but tires of them quickly. No single pleasure is enough to satisfy such an appetite for long without being replaced by another. The true measure of an appetite's strength lies not in how much pleasure a person gets from something, but in how quickly they grow tired of it.

This difference can be more clearly illustrated by representing various types of food as *a*, *b*, and *c*, each accompanied by a numerical coefficient that indicates the level of pleasure or intensity felt upon its consumption. Suppose a person with a strong appetite experiences twelve units of intensity from the first portion of food, while a person with a weaker appetite feels only eight units from a similar first portion. Because the enjoyment from each successive portion tends to decrease, we might visualize their eating experiences as follows:

For the person with a **strong appetite**, eating a single type of food (say, *a*), the progression would look like this: 12a, 11a, 10a, 9a, 8a, 7a, 6a, 5a, 4a, 3a, 2a, 1a, and then a dormant or sleepy state.

For the person with a **weak appetite**, consuming three different types of food (a, b, and c), the pattern might be: 8a, 8b, 8c, 7a, 7b, 6c, 5a, 4b, 3c—followed by the point of satiety

In the first case, the person continues eating the same food until the stomach is fully loaded and eventually falls into a drowsy state.

In the second case, the person avoids the rapid decline in pleasure by frequently switching between food types.

I have placed the point of satiety for this weaker appetite at around three units of pleasure, because such individuals tend to experience a kind of psychological reaction that cuts off their desire for more food more quickly toward the end of the meal. Admittedly, this number (three units) is somewhat arbitrary, since the weaker the appetite, the higher the threshold might be.

We now clearly see the main causes behind the weakening of human appetite. A steady, reliable food supply eliminates the old cycle of abundance and scarcity.

The widespread use of machinery and natural energy sources reduces the physical exertion previously required for survival. Well-insulated buildings, proper clothing, and accessible fuel reduce the amount of carbon-based food needed to keep the body warm.

And a broad variety of food allows each item to complement the others, so that even a small overall quantity is enough to satisfy the body's nutritional needs.

When these influences combine, they significantly affect the choices we make about different kinds of food. Of course, many interfering or "disturbing" factors slow down these shifts and blur the observable results, given the modern conditions in which people live.

Yet, with each major advancement in economic life, even those temporary disturbances—though still visible—lose some of their influence.

The enduring, foundational laws of consumption are gradually becoming clearer, steadily guiding people into better alignment with their new surroundings.

In time, our appetites too must adapt to this evolving economic environment. They will inevitably become more restrained—so that the point of satiety will be reached exactly when the body's true nutritional needs have been met.

Chapter-3
The Causes Obscuring The Primary Laws of Consumption

Why do strong appetites still seem to drive success, even when modern life should naturally weaken them? This chapter uncovers the hidden forces—migration, taxation, cheap labor, and historical habits—that mask the true laws of consumption. By exposing these distortions, it reveals why progress appears contradictory and why understanding consumption is essential for guiding civilization beyond mere production toward lasting well-being.

It has been established that a regular and varied diet, along with other factors that reduce the need for food, tends to lessen the human appetite. This, in turn, leads to the emergence of individuals with milder appetites and more subdued passions. If the point of satiety naturally aligns with the actual needs of the body, then individuals who require less nourishment should, in theory, reach fullness more quickly.

However, historical evidence does not seem to support this theory. In fact, it is the stronger populations—those with robust appetites—who have often succeeded in displacing their weaker neighbors, who had fewer material needs. And even within the more developed nations, individuals who have had sharp appetites and strong passions have often emerged as the leading figures—not just in physical endeavors but also in intellectual achievements. These and other similar observations must be acknowledged. They cannot be dismissed, but perhaps they can be understood more clearly through further analysis.

To understand why human progress seems to have taken place in contradiction to what appear to be basic laws of consumption, we must look far back into human history. Only by examining the lives and surroundings of our ancient ancestors can we hope to uncover the facts that resolve this apparent contradiction.

Primitive humans were generally lazy and would not engage in work unless they were driven to it by urgent, immediate needs. In such a setting, it was the communities with the strongest appetites that were most likely to work regularly. These people were more inclined to accept the demands of routine labor, and among them, the motivation to accumulate wealth would have emerged earlier than among populations with lesser desires.

These traits offered such a substantial advantage that the nations possessing them could easily dominate others that lacked the essential traits for advancing civilization. As long as the more energetic members of a society benefited from working more, civilization tended to progress in tandem with the survival of those who had the greatest appetites.

Those individuals whose modest needs could be satisfied by just a few hours of labor each week had to yield to others whose desires were strong enough to drive them to work long hours every day just to fulfill those needs. One of the earliest challenges in primitive society was to instill in people a level of desire strong enough to compel them to work.

Because of this, the craving for stimulants like alcohol and tobacco often had a positive role in earlier societies. The intense desire for such substances drove individuals to adopt consistent work habits in order to earn what was needed to satisfy those cravings. In this way, strong appetites—even unnatural cravings for stimulants—could benefit a developing civilization, at least during the stage when people were still forming regular habits of labor.

However, these appetites and cravings stop being helpful once increasing the number of work hours each day no longer contributes to the nation's overall productivity.

Among the more advanced races, the average person is neither lazy nor idle. In fact, his productivity could increase if he worked fewer hours. Certainly, no one would argue that a streetcar conductor, working fifteen hours a day throughout the year, would become a better man by developing even stronger appetites. His existing desires already compel him to earn his living in a way that ultimately harms his health and well-being.

Is it likely that his children will be better prepared for life's challenges than the children of a neighbor who refuses to work such long hours? Can he benefit himself or society by nurturing cravings for liquor and tobacco so intense that he is forced to add even more hours to his daily labor? For civilized people today, the issue is no longer about choosing between work and laziness. The real concern is that individuals are so eager to work that they harm themselves in the process. This self-inflicted harm weakens their children, making them less capable of thriving in the future.

The most urgent question we now face is this: what should we consume to bring about the greatest happiness in exchange for an honest day's labor? When people must choose between different sources of pleasure, possessing strong appetites offers no real advantage. Those with milder desires are now better positioned, as they are able to make wiser and more effective use of available resources.

Another major factor that obscures the natural laws of consumption is the large-scale movement of people—both from less developed to more advanced nations, and from older regions to newer ones. Most immigrants arriving in newer countries belong to that segment of the population with the strongest appetites. People do not come to America seeking more access to music, art, or similar pleasures. They come in pursuit of more food, more drink, and other material opportunities.

As a result, the national population includes a significant element that channels production and consumption in directions it might not have taken if there had been no foreign influx. The true patterns of American civilization are concealed by the presence of those who have yet to be shaped by American conditions. We seem to have developed stronger appetites than in the past, but this is merely the result of averaging together those who consume modestly and others who prioritize the satisfaction of their appetites above all else.

Even though there is a fast-growing segment of society that abstains from alcohol and tobacco, the total consumption of these substances continues to rise. Similarly, the steady movement of people from rural areas into cities helps to disguise the impact of urban environments on people's habits. City dwellers work less and rely more heavily on artificial means such as heating and clothing for protection, unlike those who live and work on farms. The continuous influx of people from the countryside masks the decline in appetite that naturally comes from adapting to city life. Once again, incorrect conclusions are drawn by combining the behaviors of new arrivals with those of families that have lived in urban environments for generations.

Additionally, the existing system of taxation plays a central role in clouding our understanding of the powerful trends currently urging individuals to adjust their appetites and change their consumption patterns. Taxation is so widely disliked that people do everything possible to shift the burden onto others or, at the very least, keep it hidden from plain view. Today, lawmakers are not tasked with minimizing the burden of taxation itself, but rather with finding ways to apply taxes in ways that go unnoticed.

As a result, the goods whose prices have decreased the most often end up bearing the heaviest tax burden. This is especially true for sugar, tobacco, and liquor—items widely considered to be luxuries. While this approach to taxation may offer some short-term advantages, it causes long-term harm. If every product were taxed by the government in proportion to its cost reduction, there would be no change in the relative prices of goods, and consumption habits would remain unchanged. Society would stagnate, missing out on the benefits that come from curbing old appetites and embracing new forms of pleasure.

It is true that taxing in this way may spare some individuals from certain new problems. However, society as a whole pays too high a price for that relief when it comes at the cost of slowing the natural and necessary evolution of civilization.

In the case of sugar, a nourishing and beneficial substance is kept out of widespread use because of its high cost. Many other foods that require sugar to be palatable are also excluded from the everyday diets of the people. As a result, individuals are prevented from gradually expanding the variety in their diets—an expansion that would naturally help reduce excessive appetite and enable more efficient use of agricultural land. If the tax on sugar were lifted, the subsequent rise in productivity would increase the income of the next generation so significantly that even ten times the current level of taxation could be collected in the future without placing any added burden on society.

Even in the case of liquor and tobacco—where the harms of increased consumption are the most obvious—society incurs substantial losses from its misguided attempts to curb their use by making them more expensive.

The craving for these substances is so intense that the only way to limit their consumption is by reducing people's incomes to the point where they can no longer afford them in large amounts. And even if this method did succeed, it would block the kind of personal development that can only occur through the natural lessening of appetite. The root of the problem lies in the strength of the appetite itself—not in the act of satisfying it. As long as the desire remains powerful, it will be fulfilled regardless of the cost to other aspects of life. Making liquor and tobacco cheaper would not increase the societal damage they currently cause. Place a man in conditions where he can obtain only half the amount of liquor he desires, and he—along with his family—will live in misery. But if he has unrestricted access to alcohol, he will eventually be forced to reform, simply in order to survive. Heavy drinking can, paradoxically, lead to no drinking at all, because the overwhelming satisfaction it brings ultimately dulls the craving and strengthens the individual's moral resistance to the habit.

Therefore, society has nothing to gain by artificially inflating the prices of liquor and tobacco. A nation can only be considered healthy when people's appetites have diminished to the point where they no longer crave such crude pleasures. High taxes may delay the self-destruction of addicted individuals, but they cannot reduce the number of people who fall victim to these habits. On the contrary, they cause further harm by masking the fundamental laws of consumption, thereby preventing the public from recognizing the only true solution to the problem.

The fourth major reason why human appetites remain so strong—despite the natural laws that should diminish them—is found in the widespread use of cheap labor that accompanies modern industrial production. The rise of machinery and the expansion of large-scale manufacturing allow employers to hire workers from much lower social and economic backgrounds than they previously could. Every time the division of labor extends into a new area of industry, many skilled workers must step aside to make room for others from less experienced or less refined labor classes.

This constant influx of the lowest tier of laborers into nearly every industry demonstrates how powerful the forces are that push employers to continuously seek cheaper sources of labor. But these lower-class workers more closely resemble primitive humans in their tendencies, and they generally possess stronger appetites and more intense passions than the workers they replace. For these reasons, the benefits of improved production appear to support the views of those economists who argue that human appetites grow stronger as civilization advances. Yet, even if we accept all the evidence on which this belief is based, we do not have to alter any of the fundamental laws of consumption that have been previously discussed. The positive effects of improved consumption cannot become evident until society has undergone the changes that naturally result from strong appetites.

The beneficial role of strong appetites in the early stages of human development cannot be overemphasized. People must first learn the habits of regular work, along with the values of saving and efficient use of resources. And nothing achieves this more effectively than having desires so powerful that they far surpass the amount of goods their labor can produce. Individuals must feel the sharp discomfort of unmet needs before they are motivated to work consistently at home or to improve their lives in new lands.

It is this intensity of appetite that drives people into jobs and places where the discomfort of labor is outweighed by the satisfaction gained from the fruits of their own production. In doing so, they gradually stop relying on nature's free offerings and begin to realize that sustained productivity is the least burdensome way to fulfill their needs. As their habits of thinking and physical strength evolve to meet these new conditions, an increasing number of goods can be produced with such ease that the effort of labor becomes less painful than the pleasure of enjoying the result. This dynamic encourages them to work longer hours—until they reach the maximum point at which labor remains efficient. Any further increase in work beyond this point becomes harmful to society. And those who suffer most from overwork are the very individuals whose appetites remain the strongest. Once this peak of labor efficiency is reached, society enters a new phase of development. At that stage, strong appetites are no longer a strength—they become a liability. The basic laws of consumption then rise to prominence as the guiding forces of progress, while the earlier disrupting influences fall back into their proper place.

In the context of American civilization, it appears that a significant segment of the population has already passed this limit of maximum labor efficiency, while another segment still relies on the powerful motivation provided by strong appetites. This creates a conflict between two distinct social groups: one group seeks to use America simply as a platform for indulging intense desires for food and drink, while the other group is striving to control its appetites and direct production toward fulfilling a broader range of emerging needs.

This conflict is part of the transitional period in which we currently live. Once this period comes to a close, we will have clear and undeniable evidence of what the actual time-limit of efficient labor is. If it is ultimately proven that working longer hours does not increase total output without harming the worker, it will also become evident that individuals driven by a deep hunger for a few specific pleasures are no longer more successful than those whose milder appetites encourage them to diversify their consumption. While we may still debate whether that limit has already been reached, there is no doubt that such a limit exists—and that our civilization is approaching it. Once it is crossed, the true laws of consumption will become just as visible in their effects on society as the current laws of production are. At that point, real-world evidence will be added to the theoretical insights we already possess, and it will become clear to all that the laws of consumption deserve just as much attention and study as those of production and distribution.

Chapter-2
The Influence of the Cost of Commodities upon their Consumption

Why don't we always consume what we desire most? This chapter reveals how cost, labor, and effort quietly reshape our choices, often overriding pure pleasure. By uncovering the hidden balance between utility and sacrifice, it shows how prices transform appetites, alter social habits, and even influence morality, health, and culture—demonstrating that consumption is governed not by desire alone, but by the economics of satisfaction.

In the previous section, I focused entirely on the factors that determine how much happiness we gain from consuming food. At first glance, it might seem that once we've measured the intensity of our desire for food and other goods, we have also discovered the rules that govern the consumption of wealth. What could seem more logical than the idea that we first satisfy those desires which are strongest? And if this is true, doesn't it follow that the intensity of each desire can be determined by the order in which we choose to consume various goods?

This line of reasoning, however, contains a major flaw. From the total intensity of any pleasure, we must subtract the pain or discomfort in any way connected to it before we can determine its actual standing among our pleasures. The urge to avoid pain influences our decisions just as strongly as the drive to pursue happiness. Our aim is not simply to obtain the most happiness regardless of cost, but rather to secure the highest *net* happiness—the greatest excess of pleasure over pain. This distinction is especially important in economics, because the wealth we consume is not nature's free gift. We enjoy only what we can produce, and that production usually comes through effort and labor. Thus, the pain of producing something directly affects our desire to consume it.

To illustrate this, imagine a person attending a lavish banquet where all the finest foods are available without cost. What would he eat first? Naturally, the items that bring him the most pleasure. Once his desire for these is satisfied—or once their utility to him begins to decline—he would turn to other foods that excite his appetite less. Because the usefulness of each additional portion drops quickly, he would end up consuming a wide variety of foods.

Now contrast this with the same person at a typical dinner he must pay for. Here, he would likely consume a completely different selection. Knowing that a certain dish he loves is two or three times more expensive than a more modest dish, for which he has only mild interest, he will likely choose the latter. Many of the costly delicacies he enjoyed in abundance at the free banquet might not appear at all in his ordinary meals. And even when they do, he would eat them sparingly.

From this comparison, we can understand that there are *two distinct orders* in which people select items for consumption. The first is the **natural order**—how people would choose goods if guided only by biological and sensory factors that make some items more enjoyable than others. The second is the **economic order**—how people choose when their natural preferences are adjusted by the effort or labor required to produce those goods.

If the labor needed to produce every item were directly proportional to the pleasure gained from consuming it, then these two orders would match perfectly. But in reality, this rarely happens. The pleasure derived from consuming the result of a week's labor in wheat production may not equal the pleasure from a week's labor in corn, rice, tobacco, cloth, or tools. Even if someone enjoys wheat more than rice, he may still choose rice if rice farming is more productive than wheat farming—so that the pleasure derived per unit of labor is higher.

Suppose that a dinner of wheat-bread brings eight units of pleasure but requires six units of pain to produce. Meanwhile, a rice dinner brings four units of pleasure and costs just two units of pain. In this case, the person would choose rice, because the *ratio* of pleasure to pain is higher. Under economic circumstances, a person will always choose first the item with the highest ratio of pleasure to pain, then proceed down the list according to descending ratios.

To restate this in economic terms: substitute *utility* for pleasure, and *cost in labor* for pain. Then we can say that individuals choose goods based on the ratio of their utility to their cost. This ratio determines the order in which commodities are consumed, and thus forms the true foundation of the laws of consumption.

It may appear a bit abstract to speak of calculating the ratio between the cost of goods and the pleasure they give us—but in practical terms, every family does this regularly. Our unit of cost is the dollar, and our measure of utility is the enjoyment we receive from a dollar's worth of a particular product.

A dollar spent on beef is mentally compared to a dollar spent on pork, mutton, cabbage, or potatoes. We don't simply pick what we like most, ignoring how much of it a dollar will buy. Instead, we hesitate, weigh our options, and decide whether a dollar's worth of one food will make a more enjoyable meal than the same dollar spent on another.

This comparison between cost and pleasure never stops influencing our decisions. Even if we never use abstract economic formulas, we are still, in practice, always weighing cost against utility.

The recent drop in the price of sugar deserves special attention because the shift is still new enough that its broad economic effects are only beginning to become clear. In the past, sugar was expensive and considered a luxury. And because of this long-standing habit, many people still treat it as one. But its price has now fallen so much that a pound of sugar costs only a little more than a pound of flour—and it's likely to become even cheaper soon. This change is likely to completely transform our current eating habits. Many fruits and vegetables only become truly palatable when sweetened, and sugar is just as important in making them usable as salt and ice are in preserving meat. Once old prejudices and habits that limit sugar use fade away, and once sugar taxes are lifted, we can expect a surge in fruit and vegetable consumption just like the growth in meat consumption that followed the widespread use of salt and refrigeration.

This surge in sugar consumption is particularly noteworthy because of its ties to the temperance movement. Historically, working-class diets were made palatable mainly through liquor. It was the enjoyable part of meals, helping to wash down coarse and poorly prepared food. Since no other satisfying and affordable diet was available, alcohol consumption couldn't easily be reduced without making meals intolerable. But now things are different. The falling price of sugar makes a pleasing diet available to nearly everyone. Today, it is far easier to convince someone to give up alcohol when there are equally enjoyable, affordable alternatives available. In fact, many people who support the temperance movement live largely on sugar-based diets—getting most of their mealtime pleasure from sweet foods. As consumers, they form a distinct group, with a completely different set of consumption patterns from those who rely on alcohol. With each drop in the price of sugar, this group gains a competitive edge in the workforce over the drinkers. It doesn't seem far-fetched to say that, eventually, the affordability of their diet could help them dominate much of the employment market.

That said, I do not claim that all the consequences of increased sugar use are positive. A rise in sugar consumption is beneficial to society overall, even though it may harm some individuals. Just as advances in production can cause harm, so too can advances in consumption. Some people's intense cravings for sweets may, without a doubt, harm their health. Cheap sugar may ultimately weed out those whose health is most vulnerable to it, leaving behind those with milder appetites. Over time, sugar might even become so harmful that people begin to view it with the same moral concern they now reserve for alcohol and tobacco. Yet even that would highlight how deeply sugar had changed our appetites through long-term use.

Alcohol, too, permanently changed the desires of those who drank it for generations. If people were to completely stop drinking, the alterations in appetite caused by alcohol would remain—but overall, society might be better off because of the lessons learned, despite the many individuals harmed along the way. Similarly, once sugar's lower price fully reshapes our collective desires, we will see another major shift in our tastes. People will become more thoughtful consumers, and because of their lighter appetites, they will seek a wider range of foods to meet their nutritional needs. Many foods that are currently only enjoyed when sweetened won't be abandoned when the craving for sugar diminishes. Instead, we'll learn to appreciate their natural flavors, and they will gradually become part of our standard diet.

Our current craving for sugar can be compared to the Eskimos' (Esquimaux's) love for fat. They drink oil with the same enthusiasm that we eat candy. Their strong preference for fat isn't surprising when we consider the harsh climate they live in and the limited range of foods available to them. Nature has had to give them an intense desire for a substance that is both scarce and vital for survival in such conditions. If their environment were to change and they had access to a wider variety of foods, their appetite for fats and oils would naturally decrease.

This strong appetite for fat is typical of primitive societies. Just a few centuries ago, fatty meat was more expensive than lean meat. Over time, however, preferences have shifted—fat has been replaced by butter, and molasses by refined granulated sugar—signaling the development of more refined tastes among modern people. Just as a new, more diverse food environment turned an affection for fat into a sense of disgust, so too are people's desires for alcohol and tobacco beginning to fade. In the future, the same decline may occur with sugar and other intense cravings.

However, it is important to remember that the relative cost of goods, as reflected by market prices, does not by itself give a complete or accurate measure of the relationship between cost and usefulness. The usefulness—or utility—of a product can shift due to factors that have no effect on its market value. For people who only think about immediate needs, cheap and low-quality items might seem more useful than they do to those who value long-term well-being. Decisions between sturdy, high-quality clothes or furniture and their flimsy imitations—items that may only serve short-term needs—depend greatly on how much consumers value their future. As people begin to care more about the long-term, their sense of utility shifts in favor of more durable items, even if those items haven't changed in price.

The usefulness of any food item also heavily depends on the cooking skills of those preparing it. In America, for example, meat and wheat bread are consumed in large quantities partly because many cooks lack the skill to make vegetables taste good. This trend becomes obvious when Americans travel to France or Germany. There, even those who would rarely eat vegetables at home begin enjoying a wide variety of them, simply because the cooking is much better. With superior preparation, dishes become far more appealing, and previous biases against certain foods fade away.

Looking ahead, true dietary luxuries won't be defined by rare ingredients, but by the skill with which meals are prepared. Nature rarely provides a simple, ready-made dish that fully satisfies our refined tastes. We need to learn to create delightful meals from humble ingredients—just as we've learned to turn cheap raw materials into high-quality goods. Skilled labor in the kitchen can increase the usefulness of food just as effectively as it can enhance the value of wool or iron. As culinary techniques improve, inexpensive foods can be used more effectively and enjoyably. Just as efficient business owners find value in low-cost labor, future cooks will find value in affordable ingredients. The plain meals of earlier generations will give way to more complex and thoughtfully prepared dishes that bring together the same nutritional components in more pleasing combinations. In much the same way that butter can be made from inexpensive sources, or olive oil from cottonseed, other expensive food products can be replicated in ways that offer the same essential nutrients—only delivered through more scientific and refined culinary methods.

There exists a common prejudice against inexpensive foods because we often associate them with a simple, monotonous way of living. In our minds, such foods symbolize a lack of variety and richness in life. We picture the New Englander eating a modest meal of corn-bread, the Irishman yearning for nothing more than his potatoes, or the Chinese content with just a bowl of rice.

Yet what often goes unnoticed is that a diet based primarily on corn, potatoes, or rice can only be sustained by those with strong appetites. It is precisely the intensity of their hunger that allows these foods to satisfy their needs. But once their appetites are diminished—due to more efficient use of the food available—these once-relied-upon staples become unappealing before they've consumed enough to meet their body's demands.

At this point, they are forced to introduce more variety into their meals. They must begin to cook with greater thought and care. The inclusion of different foods and the enhancement of cooking skills become necessary adjustments to compensate for the loss of their former appetite. However, people turn to variety and better cooking in the hope of reviving the enjoyment they once found in eating, but they do so in vain. Every new effort to increase pleasure from food through diversity and refinement in preparation only further weakens their appetite.

Once these changes begin to take hold, there is no natural stopping point. The process continues until cooking evolves into a sophisticated science, and until every piece of land is used to its fullest potential to support this intricate culinary system.

Chapter-4
The Growth of New Pleasures

How do new pleasures arise when basic appetites still rule human behavior? This chapter explores the hidden conditions—climate, environment, social structure, and cost—that allow higher enjoyments to emerge before primitive desires fade. It reveals why art, beauty, sport, and culture flourish in some societies and not others, showing how progress in pleasure follows economic and environmental pathways rather than instinct alone.

It is the most basic rule in consumption that we aim to satisfy our strongest desires first. If this principle acted alone, without help from other influences, it would not lead to the rise of new pleasures until the strength of our physical appetites had been reduced so much that greater satisfaction could be found elsewhere. In primitive human beings, the capacity for higher pleasures exists only in a basic, undeveloped form. Therefore, before those higher pleasures can begin to grow, man's more basic appetites must be reduced to their lowest point. But we are still far from reaching that point, and thus we cannot assume that the emergence of new pleasures is solely the result of a weakening in our appetites.

Even in early periods of human history, certain higher pleasures began to play important roles in human well-being. The specific conditions in different civilizations provided the circumstances under which individual pleasures could grow in strength—sometimes even surpassing the force of the primitive desires. To understand how progress has occurred, we must first identify what these conditions are that encourage the rise of higher pleasures.

One of the most powerful of these conditions comes from the irregular supply of food in the lives of early humans. The terrible effects of famine, which they experienced frequently, were never entirely forgotten during the times of plenty. The memory of past hunger created a strong desire to prepare for future security.

This very intensity of the desire for food gave birth to a new kind of pleasure—the comfort and peace that comes from knowing the future is provided for. Over time, this pleasure became strong enough to limit the careless use of present resources.

Eventually, it grew so powerful that it replaced the enjoyment of laziness and idleness with active, goal-oriented habits. These nw habits helped ease the fear of regular labor. As people became accustomed to this change, it became easier for them to endure longer periods without immediate rewards, and the pain associated with consistent work decreased.

If the initial obstacles to this transition are too extreme—as is often the case in tropical regions where nature provides too easily—then little progress is made. Only in colder climates, where nature is more challenging, do the necessary variety of conditions exist to allow gradual progress from short-term to long-term planning in consumption and effort.

Similarly, the development of aesthetic appreciation—our ability to find beauty and joy in art or form—during the early stages of civilization, when basic appetites were still strong, also depended on favorable economic conditions.

For a new faculty like this to develop, people must be led along a gradual path, step by step, requiring only minimal effort. During the early stages of this development, the environment must supply the objects of desire either completely free or at such a low cost that the effort needed to obtain them does not interfere with basic survival.

This favorable outcome can be achieved in different ways. It is not necessary that the cost of producing such articles be low, so long as the consumer is somehow unaware that they are choosing these goods over more essential ones like food. Powerful motives such as religious beliefs, national pride, or other non-economic influences often play a role in distracting attention from economic choices. This redirection of focus allows individuals to devote substantial wealth to higher pursuits—resources that might otherwise have been spent on basic needs like food or shelter—without consciously recognizing the trade-off.

This is also why the social and tribal structures of early human communities played such a vital role in the rise of new pleasures. In those societies, individuals did not act entirely on their own; they were deeply embedded in tribal relations and shared obligations.

Because of this, they did not fully feel the burden imposed by their pursuit of new pleasures. Individual self-interest was weakened by the collective nature of their society.

These larger communal structures also enabled shared enjoyment of many experiences that would have been far too costly for a single person or family to afford on their own today.

The unequal distribution of wealth, which becomes apparent early in the transition from barbarism to civilization, functions in much the same way. Those belonging to privileged classes are able to fulfill their desires and passions completely, without depleting their financial resources.

This surplus allows them to seek out new forms of pleasure—ones that are beyond the reach of others. This pursuit of exclusivity gives rise to what can be called a caste-making impulse, which proves especially beneficial for primitive societies.

When someone consumes a desirable item, the pleasure derived from using it is compounded by an added joy: the elevated social status that comes with possessing something others cannot.

This second form of pleasure—the prestige of ownership—often surpasses the original physical or emotional enjoyment of the item itself. It becomes a powerful force that restrains primitive appetites.

Without such exclusivity, the emergence of higher pleasures would have been delayed significantly. Arts such as music and literature owe much of their development to the patronage of wealthy families who used them as symbols of distinction from the common population.

In early societies, therefore, the birth of new desires was supported by many influential factors. However, it would be misleading to view these social or psychological factors as the primary reasons for their growth while ignoring the critical role of environmental conditions.

Certain pleasures can flourish only because their cost is low enough that people can enjoy them without significantly reducing their access to basic needs like food.

Climate plays a crucial role in determining whether or not specific forms of enjoyment—such as outdoor sports—can become popular. For example, had Greece been located in a region with a harsh, unpredictable climate like that of the continental interior, it would never have developed the athletic sports and public games that were so vital to its cultural evolution.

Likewise, had Athens been situated in a place like St. Petersburg, where cold and damp conditions rapidly decay marble, it is unlikely that artists would have been motivated to produce the statues for which ancient Greece became renowned.

Music, too, in its early stages, must be inexpensive to be widely enjoyed. This requires a climate in which the human voice remains clear and resonant.

A well-functioning voice—being a free instrument of high value—provides a foundation on which the musical traditions of more advanced nations could grow and develop.

However, it is not enough for a new pleasure to begin as a freely available experience. If the conditions required for its long-term development become too costly, its full potential may never be realized.

While the cost of a pleasure can increase over time as the strength of the desire grows, it must not rise faster than the enjoyment it brings. Otherwise, the foundations of future progress are undermined.

The climates of ancient Greece and Rome, for example, made it possible to host theatrical performances outdoors. Their people possessed vivid imaginations, which brought simple plays to life in ways that today can only be recreated through elaborate and expensive costumes, sets, and technology.

It's difficult to see how modern opera and drama could have evolved to their current levels without those early conditions that allowed them to begin almost without cost. Furthermore, during the stages of their artistic progression, the expense of production increased at a slower pace than the intensity of the pleasure the performances provided.

More recently, however, there are signs that this balance is shifting in the wrong direction. The cost of producing high-level performances seems to be rising faster than the value or pleasure they offer. As a result, these refined art forms now draw audiences only when they receive financial support from public funds or wealthy patrons.

If we examine American conditions, we will find that certain factors are actively promoting the development of pleasures that are inexpensive or even free to us, while slowing the advancement of other pleasures not well supported by our current environment.

Today, art and aesthetic taste enjoy special advantages that they have rarely—if ever—had before. Technological innovations have drastically lowered the cost of reproducing visual art, bringing beauty within reach of nearly everyone. Many forms of artwork have become so affordable that they are even used for advertising purposes. Across the country, even the poorest homes are filled with beautiful objects, many of which come at no cost at all. And as people's taste becomes more refined through exposure to these objects, they are able to choose others, better suited to their improved sense of beauty, with only a small increase in cost.

Advancements in machinery have also made factory-produced cloth superior to the unattractive, homemade fabrics of earlier times. With an abundance of choices in color and pattern, every person can now select what suits them best—without paying more.

These circumstances create an ideal environment for the growth of aesthetic taste, which will likely soon be strong enough to create a broad market for the finest works of art.

However, the growth of a deep love for music in America, I fear, will face significant challenges. The climate here does not seem to support the ideal use of the human voice. Moreover, the types of musical instruments capable of developing refined public taste are expensive and require great effort and time from the player to master.

The circumstances under which musical performances such as concerts and operas are held make them extremely costly, since outdoor music is impractical for most of the year due to the country's unpredictable weather.

People in rural areas, and even in many smaller cities, have almost no opportunity to experience music except in churches, where only the simplest hymns are sung. Such limited access, combined with the high cost of quality instruments, offers little hope of cultivating a widespread appreciation for music. In contrast, in the areas of dress and aesthetic taste, meaningful progress seems far more attainable.

At first, it might seem surprising to conclude that the love of music will not grow in America, especially given the high volume of musical instrument sales. The issue is not the lack of opportunity to begin musical education, but the absence of motivation to continue progressing. There is a wide gap between the simple songs heard at home or in church and the sophisticated works performed in operas and orchestras. The best music is so rarely heard—even by a small portion of the population—that it has little influence on the general public's taste. Most amateur musicians learn a few easy pieces and continue in solitude for a few years before ultimately giving up as life's responsibilities become more demanding. Unless this isolation is broken—perhaps by making concerts, operas, and other musical experiences more affordable—there is little hope for advancement in musical culture, even if every home contains a cheap organ.

That said, I do not mean to suggest that the love of music is disappearing. In fact, among a significant portion of the population, the passion for music is so strong that even today's high costs won't stop them from pursuing it.

However, it is unlikely that this love will grow among those for whom music currently holds little appeal. Like all emerging pleasures, music must be made freely available and appealing—at least initially—before its enjoyment can become widespread. Just as with other aspects of culture, our progress in music must follow the economic path shaped by our surroundings.

As a nation, we are therefore less likely to advance in music, theater, and other expensive cultural pleasures. Instead, we will find fulfillment in books, visual art, fashion, and home décor—areas where the relative cost remains much lower.

In Australia, however, a different set of conditions appears to exist compared to those in America, resulting in a distinct type of pleasures being favored. The climate in Australia is dry, with a stable and moderate temperature, making outdoor life particularly enjoyable. Because of this, there may be no other place in the world where so much emphasis is placed on all kinds of outdoor recreational activities. Australians have developed a genuine love for field sports and display a deep appreciation for athletic games. Both the people of Australia and those of the United States have inherited from their English ancestors a shared set of customs, habits, and forms of enjoyment. If not for the profound differences in their environments, these nations might have continued to develop along similar cultural lines.

However, the sudden and extreme fluctuations of the American climate have led Americans to become more inclined to indoor living. As a rule, they do not even enjoy walking as a form of exercise. In contrast, Australia's agreeable climate has encouraged its people to spend more time outdoors.

Under such differing circumstances, the character traits inherited from their common ancestors are gradually being replaced by new traits more suited to the distinct environments of each nation. As time goes on, the differences in the kinds of pleasures pursued by each nation will only become more pronounced—until eventually, their shared language may be the only real link remaining between them.

We cannot, I believe, overemphasize the importance of a nation's environment in shaping its consumption habits and sources of pleasure. Every nation tends to prefer the things its surroundings can offer with the least effort or cost.

It is no coincidence that Germans are drawn to beer and music, or that the French gravitate toward art and wine. Russia, for instance, cannot imitate either nation, even if it wanted to. Its climate poses a significant barrier to such developments and pushes its people into a different lifestyle altogether.

Even more, it is virtually impossible to transplant European customs and habits into American life. America must learn to cultivate its own inexpensive and sustainable pleasures while avoiding those that prove harmful in its unique context. Many recent immigrants try to retain their European styles of living, but ultimately, the American environment will exert too strong an influence for them to resist.

This is perhaps most clearly seen in their drinking habits. No matter how much they may cling to their beer or whiskey, they will eventually be compelled to abandon these habits if they prove harmful in the American setting.

Alcoholic beverages, no matter how well-suited they may be to certain parts of Europe, do not integrate well into American life. Instead, Americans must discover alternative ways to satisfy their thirst that align more closely with the nature of their land and climate.

That said, this challenge is far from simple. The quality of drinking water in America often falls short of the standards needed for good health. And it is unlikely that people will adopt a national drink that does not offer some real enjoyment. The human instinct to derive pleasure from everything is too strong to allow such a significant possibility to go unfulfilled. Therefore, identifying what Americans can drink—something that brings both health and pleasure while minimizing harm and disease—is just one of many complex challenges that must be solved before American civilization can truly align itself with the continent it inhabits.

Chapter-5

The Love of Home and Country

What if the greatest forces behind production are not profit or hunger, but love and belonging? This chapter reveals how attachment to home, land, and nation quietly lowers costs, sustains agriculture, and shapes lasting prosperity. By uncovering the economic power of affection, pride, and patriotism, it shows why societies flourish most when people work not only for gain, but for places they truly love.

Any explanation of the consumption of wealth, and of the motives that influence people to produce, is incomplete if it assumes that human beings work only to obtain material goods. The commercial mindset, which has become dominant over the course of this century, now so thoroughly shapes the way people think and behave that it is easy to view humanity as engaged exclusively in a pursuit of tangible results. The central question seems to be: What physical or material benefit can each person gain from their labor? The strength of this tendency has reinforced a school of economic thought that envisions a so-called "economic man," someone driven solely by a desire for material wealth. Economists who hold this view believe that such a person provides an ideal image toward which humanity will eventually evolve. This perspective is further reinforced by the rise of cosmopolitanism, which seeks to minimize the significance of national and local affiliations in favor of what are perceived to be broader, more universal concerns. Feelings of deep attachment to one's nation or local community—long recognized as powerful forces for human progress—are increasingly dismissed as outdated instincts, supposedly belonging to an inferior stage of human development that the future man must transcend.

This limited conception of economics, however, is based on a flawed understanding of human nature. The pleasures that people seek in life cannot be reduced to a single, dominant desire. Rather, the goal of civilization should be to nurture and maximize all possible sources of human pleasure. Each pleasure speaks to a different part of human character, and the most advanced societies are those that offer gratification to the widest range of human experiences. Economists, therefore, should not select one particular desire and build theories as if it were the only one that mattered. The real challenge is to determine how strong each kind of pleasure needs to be so that people can enjoy the full bounty of the earth while expending the least amount of effort. I do not object to abstract methods that highlight one motive at a time in order to understand its specific effects. But this method must be used to explore every motive—not just the craving for material wealth, as is commonly done.

It is therefore crucial to examine what role the love of home, one's local area, and one's country will play in the future. Should we expect a future where people become so cosmopolitan that they lose all emotional connection to their birthplace? Will our farms stop being personal homes and instead be rented out like commodities to the highest bidders? Or will people's emotional bond to their homes and lands grow so strong that they perform labor not merely for financial return, but out of deep love for the places where they were born? Contemporary debates touch on these questions, but rarely confront the central issue directly. They tend to take the cosmopolitan ideal as a given, then attempt to define the laws of a world where people with powerful desires and intense appetites exploit the planet solely for material purposes. Certainly, a person who is obsessed with beefsteak, beer, and tobacco will likely have little loyalty to any one place. Such a person might easily migrate to wherever these luxuries are most affordable. These are the types who would gladly displace the people of Ireland to secure beef, devastate Virginia to get tobacco, or convert India into a vast wheat field to produce cheap bread.

Yet despite the strong forces supporting such individuals, they may not be the ones who ultimately inherit the earth. In the long run, they may be replaced by people with weaker appetites—people who are more influenced by other, perhaps nobler, pleasures. This is why it becomes important to explore the possible economic value of human emotions, particularly those that bind individuals to their homes and communities. No one would deny that such feelings have played an important role in shaping history. What we need to understand now is how these emotions might continue to contribute to the progress of human society in the future.

One of the greatest obstacles to faster social progress lies in the slow growth of agricultural production. Although new areas are being cultivated and older lands are being improved, these changes are not happening quickly enough to prevent the continued high cost of food. Traditionally, the high price of food has been attributed to the greater expense involved in cultivating newer lands. However, this perspective is rooted in a misunderstanding, as the phrase "cost of cultivation" is used in two different ways. In one sense, it refers to the actual labor required to farm a field. In another, broader sense, it includes the return needed on the investment made to prepare the land for cultivation in the first place.

Once land has been cultivated, it generally remains in use as long as the returns are sufficient to cover the annual cost of farming it. For older lands, only this recurring cost is considered when calculating cultivation expenses, and any income above that is referred to as "rent." However, no one attempts to bring new land under cultivation unless the price of food is high enough to justify not only the regular cost of farming but also the cost of making the land arable in the first place. This is why newly cultivated lands end up setting the market price for food.

Older lands often generate high rents because their initial development costs are long forgotten or ignored in economic calculations. While this way of defining rent is generally accepted, it shouldn't obscure the fact that food from new lands is more expensive partly because of costs that are excluded when calculating rent on older lands. If those same costs—like clearing trees, breaking the soil, building roads, and even migrating to new regions—were factored into the cost of older land, it's likely that average farms would appear to yield no rent at all.

Carey's approach to this issue is valid. He argues that it's just as logical to include these setup costs when calculating rent for older lands as it is for Ricardo to include them when discussing newly cultivated lands. Using Ricardo's own accounting methods, Carey demonstrates that no land truly pays rent. In fact, whether society owes landowners a debt or landowners owe something back to society depends entirely on how the accounting is done. Each expense involved in making new land usable has as much claim to a return as any other. If every one of these costs were accounted for, food prices would have to be significantly higher than they are now in order to provide a fair return on the capital invested in new farmland.

No investment group or stock company could afford to develop a new agricultural region under current food prices. All ventures that have attempted this have ultimately failed—and this failure is inevitable. Even land at the edge of cultivation—often called the "margin"—has a market value far below what it cost to prepare it for use. The only reason there appears to be balance between the value of its produce and the cost of its cultivation is because of a clever form of bookkeeping. This accounting selectively includes just enough of the land development costs to match the value of its produce. When food prices rise, more of these initial costs are acknowledged in the books. When prices fall, these costs are conveniently ignored to maintain the illusion of economic balance.

The issue at hand is not merely about defining or solving the rent problem. There is another, equally important concern: What incentives should society create to motivate people to cultivate new land? And why is it that the value of land remains lower than the cost required to make it usable? Food prices are too high to suggest that they are based only on the yearly costs of cultivation, yet they are also too low to support the claim that the initial cost of making the land tillable is fully reflected in those prices.

It becomes clear, then, that commercial motives alone are not what drive people to cultivate land. Farmers do not view their land merely as a tool for producing goods or earning money. They also see it as an extension of their home—something they take personal pride in. Over time, they develop emotional attachment to their land, and a significant portion of their labor comes not from a desire for profit, but from the wish to make their surroundings more comfortable and beautiful. A farmer who owns his land does not stop working just because the financial return drops below the average wage rate. He continues working for smaller returns, or even without financial returns, simply because of the deep interest he takes in his farm.

He might invest far more than the land's market value just to remove stones or tree stumps, driven by a desire for neatness and aesthetic satisfaction. He eliminates weeds because they are unpleasant to look at, and he drains swampland not just for yield, but because he sees unproductive land as a blemish. Though these efforts do boost the land's productivity, they are better understood as acts of personal consumption—expressions of care and enjoyment, rather than just economic calculation. The farmer finds as much joy in caring for his land as he does in enjoying his meals, and he works just as earnestly for both.

This is why the value of land is often lower than the total cost of making it productive. The reason lies in the motivations behind the improvement: when people are driven by love for their home rather than financial gain, the labor they perform lowers the actual cost of food. Because their aim is not pure profit but a better life in a place they love, the total expense of bringing land into use is effectively reduced. The more farmers love their land, the closer the price of food will get to the simple annual cost of tilling the soil.

These ideas have strong implications for one of today's key debates. There are proposals suggesting that land should be taken away from individual farmers and held collectively, with farmers becoming tenants who work the land on behalf of the community. But we must ask whether such a shift would bring any real or lasting gain to society. Under a system of tenancy, the price of food would need to be high enough to make it worthwhile for an investor or capitalist to take on the task of improving and cultivating the land. Every minor task—pulling weeds, digging ditches, clearing stones—would need to be compensated at full market rates. On top of the basic cultivation cost, food prices would also need to cover the interest on the capital spent improving the land.

In contrast, if the community ensured long-term security for the farmers and nurtured their natural attachment to land and home, those farmers would likely shoulder the full cost of land improvement themselves. Society cannot simply confiscate land and expect cheap food to follow. However, it can steadily reduce its share of land development costs by placing people with strong emotional ties to the land upon it. In such cases, food prices could eventually fall to match just the recurring cost of production.

These lessons extend beyond farmland. Homes, communities, and nations should be cared for and improved not just as financial investments but as sources of emotional satisfaction. They are valuable because they bring joy, and the efforts we make to enhance them should be seen as a kind of consumption. In truth, people rarely act to improve their surroundings unless driven by love and pride. Roads, schools, and churches are seldom developed until people come to care deeply about their community. Cities only begin to feature free parks, attractive streets, and fine public buildings when their citizens take pride in their urban space and want to make it beautiful.

Even on the national scale, infrastructure such as rivers and harbors are only improved when patriotism grows strong. Forests are preserved not out of economic calculation but from a deep love of nature—a love that compels people to restore degraded lands like mountains and deserts. Commercial motives tend to exhaust the land, creating a brief period of cheap resources followed by lasting high prices caused by depleted soil. Lasting, low prices come from different impulses—especially the love people have for their land, their home, and the natural world around them.

Even the improvement of livestock is largely motivated by affection. Farmers who love their horses and enjoy working with them create the demand for better breeds. Cattle—and even pigs—can be appreciated as beautiful creatures, and much of the labor involved in raising them is done with care and devotion. It's often said of sheep that they cannot be successfully raised for profit alone. Unless the shepherd truly loves his flock, they will not thrive.

It is a mistaken belief that people should be stripped of all emotional interest in the things around them. Removing all motivations except commercial ones would not make goods cheaper—it would make them more expensive. Only among the lowest-paid laborers does the value of their output match the effort it takes to produce it. These workers find no joy in their labor and would stop working the moment their wages failed to fully compensate their effort. In contrast, people of a higher type genuinely enjoy working. They take pride in creating something well-made and in witnessing the results of their own skill and dedication.

For the general public, the real cost of what such people produce is not the full measure of their effort, but their effort *minus* the joy they get from doing it. As the pleasure of creating grows, the price of the product tends to fall below the actual labor required to produce it.

The low cost of books and literature is a clear example of this trend. Similarly, the earnings of public speakers, musicians, and artists often follow the same principle. While there are certainly exceptions—many of them well-known—these cases are typically due to the limited supply of highly skilled people. As long as there are too few individuals of exceptional talent, their work holds a kind of monopoly. But if the number of such individuals were to increase, the cost of their labor would visibly decrease.

One of the most serious flaws in economic thinking has been the separation of the laws of consumption from those of production.

Consumption is often seen only as a source of pleasure, while production is viewed strictly as painful effort. But in reality, our consumption is influenced by the varying costs of what we consume, and the cost of production—for consumers—depends heavily on how much enjoyment the producers gain from their labor. Therefore, we cannot blindly accept the rule that the value of goods depends entirely on the pain or burden of making them. For many items, their normal value will be *less* than their cost of production.

In fact, the income generated from permanent improvements—such as buildings, infrastructure, and community features—will fall as people's love for their homes and homeland increases.

When that emotional attachment reaches its highest point, people will invest in their homes, neighborhoods, and nations not for financial return, but out of genuine affection. Parks, forests, rivers, churches, and schools will then be seen as beautiful assets of communal life. The work that each generation puts into these things will not be done for money, but for the joy they provide. In this way, every new generation can inherit a world better than the one their parents knew—and enjoy it with less effort and toil

Chapter-6
The Standard of Life

What truly raises a nation's standard of life—more goods, or a deeper transformation of desire itself? This chapter reveals why lasting progress depends not on abundance alone, but on weakened appetites and diversified pleasures. It explains how stability, variety, and balanced satisfaction reshape consumption, creating resilient societies whose well-being endures even amid population pressure and economic change.

When we search for the reasons that determine people's standard of living, the first place to look is the physical environment in which they live. The first step in any effort to civilize human beings is to reduce the power of the passions and appetites that dominate their behavior.. While passions must be governed through moral discipline, appetites arise from the physical surroundings, and can only be curbed by changing that environment.

This distinction is important—it separates the economic from the moral domain. Although the two are deeply connected, real progress in either direction depends on improvement in both. There comes a point where moral restraint alone cannot work if the strength of appetites remains undiminished. On the other hand, simply weakening the appetites will not lead to a higher form of civilization unless people's passions are also brought under the guidance of moral values.

In trying to identify the economic causes that reduce appetites, the earlier discussions prove especially helpful. Chief among these is the growing consistency in the supply of food. As long as cycles of feast and famine regularly alternate, a strong appetite remains essential for survival—the ability to live through long periods of scarcity depends on having eaten heartily during times of abundance. But as the food supply becomes more stable and reliable, people with milder appetites are more likely to survive. The competition for survival starts to depend on qualities other than appetite, and a new kind of person begins to prevail—one whose actions are less driven by hunger.

This shift in appetite has far-reaching economic consequences. When appetite is dominant and remains the primary source of pleasure, people naturally tend to limit their food choices to just a few items that provide the greatest satisfaction. These intense pleasures are typically linked to rare items that nature produces only in small amounts. A strong appetite creates a preference for scarce goods. For example, the widespread demand for alcohol and tobacco keeps spending on essential items like food and clothing at low levels. Simple, nutritious vegetables are ignored in favor of meat and concentrated foods. People even reject the common cuts of meat in favor of rare portions, and they prefer wild animals over domesticated ones. In all these ways, intense appetites narrow the range of the food supply and lead to a tension between population growth and available resources.

The person whose life is ruled by animal appetites dreams of constantly indulging in rare delicacies and strong drinks. Even when forced by necessity to eat more common items, the moment their income rises, they spend the extra money not on more food or variety, but on expensive luxuries. However, as their appetites grow weaker, this problem lessens. They begin to seek out more variety in what they consume. New kinds of pleasure begin to matter more, and growing populations can be supported alongside a broader and more satisfying range of human needs.

A regular and stable supply of food is the first and most essential condition for raising the standard of living. It is the only foundation upon which the appetite can begin to lose its overpowering strength. However, once this condition is fulfilled, another factor comes into play to reinforce the same tendency—variety in food. A diverse diet contributes in the same way as a regular supply does, by weakening the dominance of appetite. But obtaining a varied diet is not as easy as it may seem.

Many writers have stressed the importance of dietary variety as a fundamental element in improving living standards. However, they often assume that people naturally move toward variety as soon as production improves. This assumption, however, is flawed. On the one hand, these writers fail to recognize that early, primitive societies tend to use their gains in production to acquire rare items that satisfy abnormal appetites in the most intense way. On the other hand, they underestimate the powerful tendency for population growth, which results in most production improvements being used simply to support more people at roughly the same standard of living as before.

As a result, we cannot accept the idea that greater production will automatically lead to a more varied consumption pattern. Some other condition must be met before we can reasonably believe that possible societal improvements will become lasting realities.

That condition lies in what might be called the economic structure of consumption. People do not always consume items in an order that brings the most pleasure first. The amount of labor it takes to produce something also affects our choices. Because labor costs influence consumption, people tend to choose items first that offer the most pleasure for the least labor. Only when multiple goods have roughly the same ratio of labor cost to satisfaction can a varied diet become permanently feasible.

In simpler terms, the standard of living can be defined as the number of different goods whose cost-to-pleasure ratios are roughly equal to those of the staple foods. So long as a dollar's worth of potatoes or rice provides twice the satisfaction of a dollar spent on other foods, most people will not maintain a varied diet. Even if a major industrial advance temporarily eases the pressure of population on food resources and creates room for more variety in consumption, that window of abundance often closes as population growth continues. Eventually, people are pushed back into the same narrow dietary habits they had before—relying once again on the cheapest staple foods.

The only way to prevent this relapse is by changing the cost-to-pleasure ratio of different foods. As long as one staple has a much lower cost per unit of enjoyment than others, there is little hope of permanent progress in dietary variety. But as soon as two or more foods offer similar value for their cost, no population pressure can force one of them out of use. In such a scenario, there is no evolutionary advantage in using just one food when other options offer the same satisfaction for the same cost. In fact, it becomes disadvantageous. When two different foods supplement each other, people can meet their needs with smaller quantities of both, achieving better nutrition and satisfaction than with a larger quantity of either food alone. For instance, if one man has a stock of potatoes and another has an equal amount of corn, both benefit from exchanging a portion of their goods.

History might have unfolded differently if this principle had applied more broadly. England was particularly fortunate in this regard. At a relatively early time—when the habits of the English people were still forming—several key food items had about the same cost-to-pleasure ratio.

Potatoes, for example, did not have the overwhelming advantage in England that they had in Ireland. Root vegetables arrived too late to significantly affect English dietary habits. The land was naturally good for growing wheat, and the lush pastures made cattle-rearing inexpensive. As a result, cattle products like beef were cheap. Poultry and eggs were plentiful, and butter cost no more than lard.

Because of these favorable conditions, all of these foods—wheat, meat, eggs, butter—became central parts of the English diet. And since their costs were low, growing populations could not displace them. Another consequence of having cheap cattle was that leather shoes became standard in England long before they did in Scotland, where cattle were less common. In contrast, the limited use of meat in Germany was largely due to the country's frequent wars, which made livestock a poor investment. Only the type of security provided by England's island geography allowed cattle to thrive to the point where meat could become a regular part of the national diet.

An increase in rent tends to encourage a greater variety in food consumption. Since rent adds a fixed cost to every type of crop, it has a proportionally greater impact on cheaper foods than on more expensive ones. For example, if ten days of labor are required to produce a certain amount of food in the form of potatoes, and twenty days for the same quantity of wheat, then an added rent equivalent to ten days of labor would double the cost of potatoes—from ten to twenty days of work. However, the same rent only increases the cost of wheat from twenty to thirty days, a rise of just one-half. This means that cheaper foods are more affected by rising rent than costlier ones, thereby narrowing the gap between them and making varied consumption more appealing or accessible.

The idea that the standard of life depends on the consistency and variety of the food supply cannot be overstated. Without recognizing this principle, no meaningful progress can be made in analyzing human consumption. An increase in the quantity of goods produced does not automatically raise the standard of living unless it also leads to increased variety in what people consume. Consider a situation where a dollar's worth of liquor or tobacco provides 20 units of pleasure, whereas the same value in food or clothing gives only 10 units, and all other commodities yield a maximum of 2 units of pleasure. In such a case, any improvement in production will merely increase the consumption of liquor and tobacco. Food and clothing would remain at their previous minimum levels, and consumption patterns would not become more diverse. To bring about a real shift in consumption, the pleasure derived from liquor and tobacco must drop to about 10 units. Only then will consumers begin to buy more food and clothing and slowly start exploring other lesser-used items. This change would broaden the standard of life, and once the variety increases, it becomes more stable—it is not easily reversed even under pressure from a growing population.

Now imagine a comparison between two individuals: the first gets 10 units of pleasure from a dollar's worth of wheat bread and only 5 units from rye bread; the second gets 8 units from wheat bread and 7 from rye bread. If their incomes were to rise, the first person would not change their diet—wheat bread still offers far more pleasure than the alternative. The second person, however, would begin to include rye bread in their consumption, as the marginal pleasure from additional wheat bread would fall below the satisfaction rye bread could offer.

As food becomes cheaper, the standard of living always improves—*if* there exists another food item not yet consumed that offers nearly the same level of pleasure as current choices. Suppose a dollar's worth of wheat bread gives 10 units of pleasure, rye bread offers 9, Graham bread 8, and corn bread 7. In this situation, every increase in income leads to greater variety in the kinds of bread consumed.

A person with such a balanced appreciation would spend extra income very differently from someone who receives 20 units of pleasure from wheat bread and less than half that from any other type. The latter would stick to wheat bread; the former would explore.

It's important not to undervalue the role of moral motivations or production improvements in lifting the standard of life. These forces push society forward and enable progress. However, that progress will not become permanent unless it is paired with an increase in the variety of consumption. Moral effort and innovation may open the door, but it is a diversified consumption pattern that ensures the door stays open and doesn't swing shut again.

A varied consumption is the anchor that keeps progress stable. Without it, society may easily revert to earlier, less developed conditions once external pressures—like moral drive or technological advancement—relax.

In this sense, a nation that relies on just a few intense pleasures resembles a tree with a single deep taproot. Meanwhile, a nation with many equally satisfying sources of enjoyment resembles a great oak tree with hundreds of roots spreading in every direction. When the winds of hardship blow, the difference in their ability to remain standing is as dramatic as the difference in their root systems.

A diversified pleasure structure gives a society the resilience it needs to resist sliding backward into deprivation.

The reduction in appetite that comes with an increased variety of consumption compels consumers to seek out new sources of enjoyment to compensate for the diminished pleasure of familiar ones.

Simply increasing the quantity of goods already in use does not have this transformative effect. Such a rise in quantity can easily be erased by economic hardship or rising population pressure, since it does not alter the underlying appetites of those consuming. In contrast, dramatically reducing a consumer's variety in food would have a severe effect.

A weakened appetite—shaped by a diverse diet—might fail before the body's nutritional needs are met. For instance, Irish immigrants in America cannot be forced back to the potato-based diet of their ancestors without causing serious harm to their health and well-being.

Likewise, the American population could not be restricted to a diet of corn bread and cabbage without suffering a major decline in vitality and efficiency. Such a drop in vitality would likely double the death rate, while the loss of productivity would lead to greater reliance on imported foreign labor.

If future workers in America were to subsist solely on cheap, coarse foods, they would not be descended from today's American population, but from the lower-income groups of Europe and Asia.

It is far easier to bring in a new class of low-wage laborers than to push the existing, more established population down to a lower standard of living.

The foundation of a nation's standard of life should now be clear. Economists have too often treated old pleasures as fixed, hoping that improvements in production would allow less intense pleasures to be satisfied, thereby elevating social standards. They have largely ignored the diminishing intensity of familiar pleasures and the emergence of new ones, which together create a continuously expanding set of pleasures with similar costs per unit of enjoyment. It is not rising income alone that allows new wants to be fulfilled.

Rather, the weakening of older pleasures—caused by varied consumption—pushes individuals to find new sources of enjoyment to make up for what has been lost.

A high standard of living is closely linked to having a weaker appetite. It is not the simple abundance of consumable goods that defines an elevated lifestyle, but the psychological condition that allows for diverse consumption patterns. The standard of life is shaped not by how much a person can enjoy, but by how quickly he tires of a single pleasure.

To have a high standard means enjoying something deeply, but growing bored of it quickly. Any pleasure becomes dull unless it can be set aside to make room for something fresh. Only through a long succession of diverse pleasures can life become truly desirable for someone whose primitive appetites have faded and now rank below other aspirations. No single new pleasure can fully replace a lost appetite. Instead, the individual can build a greater sum of happiness only by learning to enjoy a wide range of things, tapping into the many gifts nature has to offer.

From this perspective, a nation has nothing to fear in terms of a reduced standard of living—unless there is a significant shift in national industries that allows cheap foreign labor to be brought in from regions where these newer, more diverse patterns of consumption have yet to take root. In such a scenario, a lower social class might replace a higher one within certain sectors.

However, this displacement does not mean that the higher class disappears; it simply shifts. These individuals are pushed into other industries that demand more energy or into regions where the nation's natural resources are still underdeveloped. Currently, nature and land are so inefficiently utilized that someone driven by unsatisfied needs can usually find a place where their lifestyle can still be maintained. Moreover, such individuals possess the ability to reshape their consumption habits to fit their circumstances more precisely. As their appetites weaken, they find it easier to overcome the mental and cultural barriers that once kept them from embracing more affordable kinds of food.

It is, moreover, impossible for a man with a weakened appetite to go back to the coarse and limited diet of his ancestors. The food they once found acceptable is now repulsive to him, and his body can no longer tolerate it in the quantities needed to sustain physical health or mental clarity.

If the future of the world depends on people who can survive on such a diet, then neither he nor his family will remain a part of that world for long. Should competition grow too intense, he might choose to harm himself through overexertion, reduce the size of his family, or even avoid marriage altogether.

However, there is no real risk that he will willingly return to a diet he finds revolting or fall back into a way of life that no longer brings him any sense of joy.

Chapter-7
The Best Use of Land

Why does land grow scarce and food remain costly, even in an age of progress? This chapter reveals how human desires—especially what and how we consume—shape land use, rent, and productivity. By linking appetite, self-control, and capital to the efficiency of land, it shows why the future belongs to those who use limited space wisely and sustainably.

We cannot fully understand the effects of changes in consumption unless we also examine how they affect land and its rental value. The amount of usable land in a nation is limited, while human wants are so material in nature that fulfilling them inevitably places a high demand on land through its products. When we eat, drink, or clothe ourselves, we are consuming goods that require a certain amount of land for their production. If we fix the amount of land each person needs to satisfy their wants, we can then also fix the number of people that a given area of land can support.

For example, if it takes fifteen bushels of wheat to produce enough bread for one person for a year, and if one acre of land yields fifteen bushels of wheat, then it is clear that each person would require a full acre to meet their needs. If a person only has access to half an acre, they must grow something more productive than wheat, or else they will face hunger. As long as the community continues to rely solely on wheat, we can determine with certainty how many people the land can support—no more than one person per acre. Now, if the community starts using one-sixth of its land to grow tobacco instead of wheat, the number of people the land can support is reduced by one-sixth. Should they also develop a taste for beer and dedicate another sixth of the land to growing barley and hops, then one-third of the total population would be displaced compared to what it was before these new habits emerged.

This principle holds true even when different crops are grown. An acre of land can only yield a certain amount of rye, corn, or potatoes.

And since crop yields are determined by the soil and available methods of cultivation, an acre of land can only support a fixed number of people under given conditions. In essence, population grows whenever societies shift toward more productive crops, and it is restricted whenever preferences shift toward rare or luxurious goods that take up more land for less essential benefit.

In the early stages of civilization, the land problem is typically the most critical issue. Even primitive societies have non-material wants that the land cannot fulfill; but because the products of the soil meet nearly all of their basic needs, there is no significant competition among them except for the possession of land. If the population grows beyond what the land—cultivated in a crude, early manner—can sustain, then the only solutions available are war, starvation, or migration.

As population increases, people must adjust their wants. Traditional desires must become less pressing than new ones that require less land to satisfy. For instance, a tribe of hunters may require several thousand acres per person to hunt enough deer or buffalo to feed a family. When their diet changes from wild game to domestic animals, they need only a quarter of that space for grazing livestock.

As they move from herding to cultivating the soil for grain, their land needs decrease even more significantly. Each transition reflects a shift in desires and habits, and each brings a substantial reduction in the amount of land required per family.

In every era, population growth and production improvements have followed this pattern: a change in the demand for food. As the craving for one type of food fades—or at least becomes relatively less important—a new type takes its place, one that allows land to be used more efficiently.

There is a deeply rooted connection between what people desire and how much land they require. Only when people develop a preference for simpler, less expensive food can the conflicts between individual interests be reduced.

As civilization advances, we are increasingly required to adapt our lifestyles—especially in the ways we eat, drink, and dress—so that we make a smaller claim upon the land. Every family must learn to live on a smaller piece of land, adjusting their diets in a way that their needs can be satisfied within these limitations.

Because of this, the laws of consumption are crucial to understanding the direction in which population pressure pushes the development of humanity. Individuals or communities that cling to an excessive craving for rare or luxurious food items must inevitably give way to those who are content with foods that nature provides in greater abundance. Families that limit their choices because of habit, taste, or personal preference are often surpassed by those who are better aligned with nature's offerings and find pleasure in a wider variety of foods.

Strong appetites restrict diets to only those items that most intensely gratify hunger. Meanwhile, weaker appetites tire more quickly of any one kind of food and therefore require a broader mix in order to eat enough to meet physical needs. These families, with their broader preferences and lower intensity of craving, are more naturally aligned with improved methods of production and can better take advantage of nature's ability to offer variety. Any piece of land is more efficient when used to grow several different crops than when forced to produce a large quantity of just one or two. In this sense, survival increasingly favors those who enjoy all kinds of food over those who desire only a few rare ones.

There is another serious problem associated with intense land demand—it causes rent to rise significantly. Rent is not a fixed figure based solely on population size or the amount of land under cultivation. Instead, rent is paid by consumers not because they eat simply to live, but because they live to eat. There is plenty of food available at low production cost—if only consumers would treat food as a basic necessity and not the main source of pleasure.

People with strong appetites tend to narrow their food choices to those that satisfy their most intense cravings. This leads to higher prices for the few desired items—like wheat, tobacco, and livestock feed—which might otherwise be available for much less. Farmers are then compelled to grow these high-demand crops more frequently than would be ideal for their land. Other parcels of land, which are better suited for different types of crops, are underutilized because the market rewards only those crops with inflated prices. This lopsided demand shrinks the effective area of a nation's land and reduces overall productivity. As a result, the demand for food increases much faster than the supply, and the rising food prices take a significant share of industrial output away from producers and redirect it to landowners as rent.

The rise in rent stems from our personal preferences. There is no natural reason why food production must grow more slowly than population. The apparent struggle between people and their food needs arises because so many choose narrow pleasures—pleasures that exclude others. When someone enjoys a loaf of bread or a glass of beer, they do so at the exclusion of others. For more people to share in those pleasures, new bread and beer must be produced for each person. These exclusive pleasures intensify competition and raise the rent of land to the point where wages can only support bare subsistence.

This kind of conflict among people—rooted in mutually exclusive pleasures—can only be softened by the emergence of shared pleasures, those that multiple people can enjoy simultaneously without lessening anyone's experience. For example, a printer can increase the number of books or newspapers in an edition with little added cost, allowing many to read and enjoy them together. Similarly, it cost the King of Bavaria just as much to attend an opera alone as it would cost thousands of people to enjoy it together, assuming none of them felt the need to exclude others from the experience.

By shifting toward pleasures that are inclusive and broadly sharable, society can reduce the pressure on land, lower rents, and create a more balanced and equitable distribution of the resources that sustain us.

In discussions about rent, far too much focus has been placed on physical causes. It may indeed be true that the rent of a piece of land can be measured by comparing its fertility to that of the poorest land still in use. Yet we must ask: why is that poorer land still in cultivation? Is it not because the pleasure people derive from the food grown there equals the pain or effort required to produce it?

If the pleasure people get from food were to decline, this land would no longer be used. Instead, a more productive field would now become the least valuable in use, since the satisfaction from consuming its crops would merely balance the effort needed to grow them. On the other hand, if people's appetites increase, even less fertile fields will come into cultivation, because the added effort becomes worth it to satisfy stronger desires.

Therefore, the rise in rent is directly tied to the strength of appetite. If people live in an environment where those with stronger appetites have an advantage, rent will steadily rise. But if the environment favors people with more moderate desires, rent will fall each time those with a taste for exclusive pleasures lose ground. Rent, in fact, reflects differences among people more than differences among fields. If everyone had just enough appetite to meet their physical needs, no one would need to pay rent. These individuals could be called "no-rent men." Any rent paid by others would measure the extent to which their appetites exceed those of the no-rent individuals. As the gap between people with stronger and weaker appetites widens, so does rent. And if that gap narrows, rent must decline.

This is not to suggest that people with the weakest appetites are necessarily better in any social or moral sense. They are simply used here to demonstrate the idea that if rent must be understood in terms of differences, then human differences offer a more accurate measure than land differences.

Choosing the right things to consume is just as crucial to making the best use of land as choosing the right way to produce them. We often speak of production tools like knowledge, skill, and capital as if they exist outside of people, as purely objective things. Capital, especially, is usually viewed as a physical object essential for efficient production. But what really makes production efficient is how that object is used. Labor and capital are not fundamentally different things; they are simply different paths to the same goal. When labor is embodied in a material object, that is merely one kind of labor.

Let's say a man wants meat, which he cannot get without hard effort. If he chooses one method, we call it labor; if he chooses another, we call it capital. Suppose he goes out hunting wild animals—then his exertion is called labor. But if he raises cattle to ensure a steady supply of beef, the outcome of his earlier efforts, which he doesn't immediately consume, is called capital. These cattle are not capital merely because they are physical things, but because they represent a sequence of actions directed toward a consistent food supply.

This sequence of actions by the cattle herder differs from that of the hunter mainly in duration. Both types of work involve pain and effort, so they belong to the same overall category, but they differ in kind. The hunter's effort is almost entirely physical strain. The herder, however, experiences two types of discomfort: the physical fatigue like the hunter, and the discomfort of abstaining from eating his cattle until they mature. This abstinence requires self-control, which is especially painful for someone who has not developed such discipline. The stronger a person's appetites and impulses, the harder self-control becomes—and the more likely that person is to choose production methods that require only short bursts of labor.

For such individuals, physical exertion is less unpleasant than the effort of restraining themselves. Therefore, they lean toward forms of production that can be completed in a brief series of actions, avoiding long-term strategies that require patience, planning, or deferred gratification.

As human beings evolve, they begin to value the idea of securing their future. This brings about a new kind of pleasure, and with the weakening of appetite, the struggle for self-control becomes less intense. As a result, people are willing to undertake longer sequences of effort in production—leading to the rise of what we know as capital. Yet, it is a mistake to think of capital as something external or entirely separate from the labor that creates it. At the subjective level, labor and capital are simply different types of difficult efforts. Both involve exertion and both result in tangible outcomes. Even the shortest effort we classify as labor brings about visible change. It's not scientifically accurate to treat the longer forms of effort as a separate category just because their outcomes are more durable. In fact, there are even longer series of efforts that produce not goods, but greater skill and knowledge. For example, a determined effort to educate a population stretches over more years than any campaign to improve land or boost the supply of goods.

If we view these extended efforts from an external perspective, we may call all of them capital. In this way, skill and knowledge become forms of capital invested in people, just as other kinds of capital are invested in land. From a subjective standpoint, we may interpret all these efforts as different forms of skill. Skill, after all, is simply the ability to save muscular effort, and a skilled person often relies on tools or resources to reduce the need for physical exertion.

This leads us to recognize that there are many different paths by which people extract food from the land. The way a society uses its land is shaped by how unpleasant it finds muscular fatigue compared to the pains of abstinence and self-control. When people find it harder to practice self-control than to do physical labor, much of the land remains unused in any meaningful way, and the part that is used doesn't yield much. But when a group of people comes along for whom self-control is less painful, they choose to pursue longer, more sustained production efforts—often involving capital—and the land becomes more productive.

Now consider a group of people who dislike saving and gaining skill more than they dislike physical labor. These individuals will cultivate land that yields a low return and work it in ways that reduce its productivity with each additional effort. But if a new group settles in the same area—one that finds self-restraint and long-term planning easier than manual labor—they will stop working the low-yield fields. Instead, they'll focus on land where success depends more on skill and capital. This shift leads to better use of the land, and more of it becomes productive. If we add the fact that such individuals also tend to have weaker appetites—and thus require a more diverse diet—we can clearly see how the development of individuals is closely tied to more efficient land use.

This illustrates how the law of diminishing returns is deeply connected to human choices between different types of pleasure and pain. The obstacles to productive output are easier to understand when we rank people based on their economic choices rather than ranking land by its fertility. This so-called law isn't fundamentally about land, but about the people who work the land. A person who invests more in capital and skill than in raw labor will always achieve a higher return relative to the total effort. It isn't the spread of poor-quality land that reduces average labor returns—it's the overuse of less capable individuals. We need not worry about an increase in poor land—its supply is fixed and actually shrinks with every rise in capital and skill. If only we could say the same about less developed people, we'd have little to fear about the future. It is this group that truly holds back progress, preventing the kind of land use that could offer abundant and varied outputs with minimal effort.

If we thoughtfully connect the facts discussed, we will find the key to understanding why land is often misused and why food remains expensive. Individuals with strong appetites inherited from primitive ancestors are still so numerous that they create overwhelming demand for land, driven by their craving for rare foods and stimulating drinks. The same tendencies also slow down the accumulation of capital—an essential requirement for transforming poor-quality land into fertile ground. As a result, a much larger area must be cultivated than would otherwise be necessary. And because this inferior land is farmed without sufficient capital, food prices stay high. These higher costs divert much of the industrial output from the workers into the hands of landowners as rent. Expensive food is the result of poor land usage, while cheap food is a sign that limited land is being used efficiently.

Because of these realities, the public has a primary and legitimate interest in how land is used—and, in turn, a rightful authority to limit those forms of consumption that increase the demand for land and degrade its fertility. The widespread use of alcohol and tobacco, for instance, leads to entire states diverting land from its most valuable uses. In many cases, the soil is exhausted and rendered useless due to the depletion of its productive elements. The simple waste of land is harmful, but even more damaging is when land that could be used to feed or support communities is turned to less necessary purposes, scattering the population across vast spaces and isolating them from the benefits of modern life.

This public interest in land use is not a new or radical idea. As a society, we already accept that certain actions affecting the land must be regulated for the common good. We would not permit someone to block our rivers or stop the building of railroads just to prevent public access to newer states. Similarly, we object when Western cattle barons enclose massive tracts of land solely for their own gain. While there is certainly a need for beef, it is far less important than the need for affordable, basic food—and beef production should not stand in the way of better, more equitable land use. Consider also the public outcry when settlers were denied entry into the Oklahoma territory because Native Americans were not cultivating the land. If we are unwilling to let cowboys and Native communities keep others out of underutilized land, we certainly shouldn't let the indulgent habits and instincts of our less disciplined citizens waste much larger areas and make the rest of the land harder for others to use effectively—whether for public infrastructure or private livelihood.

The demand for land that arises from the dietary habits of various groups within a nation plays a crucial role in determining which class will be pushed aside as the population grows. Historically, hunting societies have never stood a chance against cattle herders, and those herders, in turn, were easily displaced by farming communities. Among more advanced societies, those who use land most efficiently inevitably gain the upper hand. A family that needs twenty acres to meet its dietary needs cannot compete with one that manages the same with ten. As population density increases, each family's available land shrinks, making it necessary to grow more productive crops. Consequently, the share of rare and extravagant foods declines, and the overall variety of consumption improves.

This dynamic will ultimately determine the outcome of the growing struggle between temperance advocates and supporters of alcohol and tobacco.

Those who abstain from intoxicants place far less demand on the land than those who indulge in these luxuries. Not only do users of liquor and tobacco require twice as much land per person, but they also face double the temptation to squander their income. Over time, those who abstain will steadily acquire a greater portion of the country's land and capital, pushing the drinking classes into lower-tier jobs—positions that offer less economic mobility and slower population growth. There is no feasible path for drinkers and smokers to maintain their position while burdened by the economic consequences of their lifestyle choices.

The temperance population will grow in both number and wealth until they become powerful enough to either marginalize or completely suppress the opposing group. Their economic advantage is just as significant as the shift from the hand loom to the power loom or from the canal to the railroad. The final result of this struggle is not in doubt. The only real question is whether users of intoxicants will be compelled to reform—or whether they will simply be overwhelmed and displaced under the weight of their own growing disadvantages.

Chapter-8
The Outlook for the Future

Is the future shaped more by machines and markets—or by how we choose to live and consume? This chapter looks beyond production to reveal how habits, desires, and education determine human progress. It explores whether society will be ruled by cheap labor and primitive appetites, or guided toward a higher standard of life through wiser consumption, adaptation, and collective responsibility.

If the analysis of consumption has been correctly made, then the real barriers to rapid human progress do not lie in our current environment. Rather, they stem from the internal habits and instincts of people, which were shaped long ago in a very different world. Human nature became so well adjusted to its earlier environment that it now clings to old ways and is skeptical of anything new. The emotional attachments and pleasures inherited from our ancestors do not adapt as quickly as our productive abilities have. As a result, there's a mismatch between our internal makeup and our external world. We may have built ourselves a new mansion on a hill, but we still prefer the old cottage in the valley. We know how to produce many new and useful things, but we still want to live much like our forefathers did. We're eager to make the new because it requires less effort, yet each of us also expects the economic system to somehow give us the rare comforts of the past in exchange for the abundant conveniences of the present.

Thus, the true obstacles to progress lie within us, not outside of us. The land could offer a far greater yield if people were willing to adjust both their production methods and their consumption habits in ways that would extract the highest value from it. But for most people, their powerful appetites limit the optimal use of land, and the pain of abstaining from gratification is greater than the pain of physical labor. As a result, they avoid those forms of work that require long-term effort and discipline. In doing so, they miss out on many labor opportunities that would offer higher returns and prevent society from gradually evolving toward a better condition. Such individuals are what we might call "cheap men," not because they earn little, but because their tolerance for hard labor is high while their appetites are strong. They are willing to toil endlessly for small amounts of food, and as their numbers grow, they create an overwhelming demand for land.

In contrast, the desires of more progressive individuals grow faster than the efficiency of their labor. As a result, even though they are more capable, they often have less surplus income to offer as rent. Rent, after all, can only be paid from the income that remains after a person has satisfied their standard of living. In this way, cheap labor becomes an obstacle to the progress of more advanced groups, because it drives up food prices. And this obstacle is made worse by the rise of a class of capitalists who provide funding at low interest rates. Modern industries combine the cost advantages of cheap labor and low interest, leading to inexpensive products and inflated rents. Cheap goods inevitably cause high rents when the laborers who produce them spend most of their earnings on food. These industries minimize the need for skilled labor and continuously find new ways to utilize even lower-skilled individuals. Ironically, this improved production system reinforces the primitive appetites and base pleasures of working men, especially when their labor is directed by a well-capitalized intellectual elite.

If we were to search for answers solely in the area of production, we might be led to the troubling conclusion that the survival of the fittest now favors the cheapest man. This is the so-called "iron law of wages," a concept that has been forcefully argued and supported by considerable evidence. But this conclusion is flawed if the laws of consumption are considered an essential part of economics. Once we identify the trend of competition in production, we only have one side of the broader equation. It certainly matters who has the upper hand in production, but it is even more crucial to understand who holds the advantage in consumption. While the more refined classes cannot offer higher rents than the lower classes, they *can* avoid paying rent altogether by consuming goods that allow for a better use of land.

If the superior man chooses to compete with the inferior one by using his income to satisfy the same base appetites, he is at a disadvantage. He only gains a competitive edge when he reshapes his consumption habits and learns to find joy in pleasures that go beyond mere appetite. But this shift is not immediate—it unfolds slowly over time. The changes in production happen quickly and are easily visible, while changes in consumption are so gradual and subtle that they often go unnoticed. It may take many generations for consumption habits to evolve in ways that correct the negative effects of rapid shifts in production. Yet these slow, quiet forces of change in consumption never stop working. Eventually, equilibrium will return, and those who adapt their consumption most wisely will rise above the rest by making the best and most efficient use of the land.

One of the most significant consequences of improved production has worked to the advantage of the more progressive classes. In earlier times, the consumption habits of each community were almost entirely dependent on the goods that could be produced locally. Consequently, the standard of living was restricted to the limited number of items that could be made inexpensively in one's own region. However, the dramatic reduction in transportation costs has made many other products just as affordable as local ones. As a result, consumption patterns have improved across all social strata, desires have become more diverse, and this shift has helped to prevent the decline in wages that might otherwise have resulted from the replacement of skilled workers with cheaper labor in large-scale industries.

Enhanced consumption also plays a role in sustaining wage levels, even amid the downward pressures exerted by more efficient production methods. It does this by triggering forces that eventually lead to the decline of the most economically vulnerable individuals.

While these "cheap" workers benefit from the nation's most skilled minds organizing and guiding them in the workplace, they are left completely unguided when it comes to how they consume. In their new living and working environments, they often neglect their long-term well-being in favor of short-term gratification. Their instincts—once well-suited for more primitive conditions—no longer serve to protect them from self-harming behaviors.

These individuals tend to live in overcrowded tenement buildings, show little concern for hygiene and sanitation, and are indifferent to the quality and safety of their food. This disregard leads to poor health, reduced physical resilience, and higher mortality rates, especially among their families. The shortsightedness of employers, who often place them in unhealthy working conditions, only adds to the harmful circumstances surrounding them. Moreover, their growing addiction to alcohol and tobacco displaces healthier forms of enjoyment and compels them to reduce both the quantity and quality of their food and clothing just to satisfy these destructive cravings.

This situation is analogous to the exploitation of cheap land—cheap labor is used in a similarly wasteful and predatory manner. The long-term welfare of the lower classes holds little value for those who benefit most from their work and spending habits. Employers overwork them; landlords deprive them of fresh air and sunlight; taverns encourage a thirst for alcohol; grocers sell them adulterated food; and merchants hide defects in their merchandise using cheap, often toxic dyes. This entire network of exploitation accelerates the decline of the lowest classes and shortens the period during which they might have continued to be economically useful, had their needs been approached with a more far-sighted vision.

The impact of improved consumption will either uplift or eliminate laborers, depending on the quality of their choices within this new framework. Some will continue to chase immediate pleasure, and by doing so, place themselves in environments that hasten their destruction and that of their families. Others will learn to adapt their desires to the changing conditions, and by doing so, will avoid many of the harmful effects experienced by their peers. Together, these dual tendencies gradually raise the general standard of living. The most vulnerable portion of the laboring class eventually disappears, leaving behind no descendants to inherit their traits. What remains is a laboring population composed entirely of those who were better able to adapt—now representing a more diverse and elevated standard of life.

The trend of improved production replacing more skilled workers with cheaper laborers aligns with a long-term rise in the general standard of living. Employers will always look for the least expensive workers, but the cheapest worker of one era is typically more capable than the cheapest worker of the era before. With every advancement in production methods, a larger proportion of lower-cost labor will likely be employed. However, it is important to recognize that the very development of the cheaper man is what enables him to replace his superior. The tendency to use lower-cost workers becomes a lasting problem only when the environment supports the survival of a lower class.

If laborers were isolated in rural areas, where access to clean air and sanitation mattered little, and where consumption remained simple and unvaried, then even the most inferior individuals could survive and raise healthy families. Under such conditions, improved production—especially if it didn't involve the expansion of industrial scale—might result in a lasting decline in the standard of life. However, large cities do not provide such protected environments. Urban life brings with it temptations, illnesses, and a wide range of consumption options. In these settings, individuals either degenerate or improve. Those who fall into disease and vice are eventually swept away, while those who adapt and evolve are left to benefit from the improved consumption possibilities.

The progressive advancement of nations—even if it involves the gradual self-destruction of their lowest classes—cannot be discredited by examples from traditional societies in places like China or India. In these regions, low-cost laborers manage to survive because they are shielded from disease by a pleasant outdoor lifestyle and protected from temptations like alcohol and opium through their societal isolation. Their deep-rooted customs and social systems insulate them from both the dangers and opportunities of modern life. The very walls that keep progress out also delay decay. But once those barriers are dismantled, individuals are free to choose their own path—toward health or toward vice. The weak are eliminated, and the capable go on to shape a new society better suited to modern conditions.

The opposing forces that arise from the simultaneous progress in production and consumption may benefit from clearer illustration to fully grasp their effects. Imagine a series of standards of life represented by the letters a, b, c, and so forth, with a representing the highest standard. As production becomes more advanced and mechanical, it tends to favor less skilled labor. Consequently, the standard of life begins to decline. Suppose it starts at point d and slowly moves downward through e and f until reaching .

However, once the benefits of improved consumption begin to assert themselves, a new and opposite force comes into play.

Workers with a g-level standard of life will either rise and adopt the f-level standard, or they will succumb to the negative effects of the new consumption options and eventually die out. The standard of life, then, stabilizes at level f, and wages rise to match this new baseline. With the next significant improvement in consumption, workers at level f will again face two outcomes: they will either be overwhelmed by the temptations of their new consumer environment and perish, or they will grow and evolve until level e becomes their new standard of living.

At each step, employers may attempt to bring in labor from regions where these transformations in consumption have not yet occurred. Nevertheless, with every advancement in consumer habits, a similar pattern unfolds. The most vulnerable are pushed out by unhealthy choices and environments, while the more adaptable climb the social ladder into higher levels of living. This ongoing dynamic steadily elevates the quality and diversity of the labor force.

If it weren't for the ongoing migration of laborers, the effects of improved consumption would quickly become visible. But the lasting problems of improved production stem largely from this very migration. Less developed regions continually send waves of laborers into the great industrial centers, where they displace established workers or, at the very least, suppress their wages. In such circumstances, the positive influence of better consumption habits unfolds only slowly, as the newcomers experience the full impact of their new surroundings only after several generations. Often, just when a group begins to demand higher wages due to improved standards of consumption, they are replaced by a new class of immigrants.

Even in this difficult scenario, however, the future is not without hope—though the time required for any significant uplift in the condition of the working class is certainly extended. A permanent resolution to these challenges will only be possible when advanced production methods are implemented in the very countries from which these laborers migrate. When every nation gives up its insular habits and guarantees security of property and personal freedom—conditions essential for adopting the best production techniques—then each country will be able to employ its own labor force within its own borders. The source of cheap labor will then dry up, and the principles of consumption will no longer be obscured by the continual importation of low-cost workers.

The fact that improved production eventually corrects its own harms does not free society from its duty to support that progress.

The natural spread of advanced production methods, even in the best case, takes a very long time, and this period can be considerably shortened through intelligent and purposeful action.

Furthermore, natural evolution is an unfeeling process: it preserves the strong and eliminates the weak. The man of the future will need to be highly skilled, disciplined, frugal, far-sighted, and possess a strong love of home, nature, and long-term well-being. Those who embody the most of these qualities will outcompete their weaker counterparts, forcing them into living and working conditions that sap their vitality and expose them to disease and moral decay.

Without assistance from society, today's lower classes will be crushed under these forces, and the world will be populated only by the descendants of those who possess the widest range of productive traits. Such a gradual change, dragging slowly over generations, will likely generate considerable tension between social groups—especially if immigration of low-wage laborers remains unchecked.

When society chooses to assist the development of the lower classes—rather than allowing them to be destroyed by the brutal forces of natural selection—the motivation should be love for humanity, not merely the practical demands of progress. There is no fear that civilization will stop evolving; the real challenge is to shorten the painful transition period and bring as much of the existing population as possible into harmony with the modern world.

It is also important to recognize that the working classes today have a just claim upon society's support, as their progress is more obstructed than it once was.

In the past, when land was cheap and production operated on a smaller scale, labor and thrift could bring quick rewards. Small producers could more easily find productive opportunities that developed their talents and improved their position. Today, it takes a far more capable person to recognize and seize such opportunities and to move from the laboring class into the ranks of employers.

In the realm of consumption, too, progress has become more difficult. Harmful pleasures—like drinking, smoking, and other distractions—have become cheaper and more accessible. Meanwhile, the higher forms of enrichment—such as music, art, and education—have become more expensive. The basic standard of living for the lowest classes has not risen; in fact, the gap between them and the higher classes continues to widen, and is becoming increasingly difficult for individuals to cross.

These individuals are, in effect, cut off from the chain of ever-growing pleasures that helped the upper classes rise from lower states. The early steps on the natural ladder of betterment—the ones the upper classes once climbed—have been broken by the very progress that raised them.

Society must now rebuild those steps if it wants the lower classes to improve in the same way. People with strong passions and desires will not shift their consumption habits unless the first steps toward better living are made freely available. When the upper classes were in the mental and emotional state that today's lower classes are in, their surroundings offered them simple pleasures at no cost, helping them progress naturally. But in today's world, those same pleasures are costly and won't be chosen unless society actively teaches people to value them. The farther modern society drifts from the primitive conditions of its ancestors, the more effort it must invest to carry its weaker members across that widening gap—if they are to be molded into a healthy and evolving part of the social fabric.

All our religious institutions, for example, trace their origins to times when religious instruction was available at no cost.

The State itself supported established churches, while dissenters—those who broke from dominant religious bodies—conducted their worship in homes, or even outdoors in the woods. Many of the newer religious sects also arose under similar modest conditions. The very term "camp-meeting" reflects how inexpensive and accessible the early gatherings of the Methodists were.

Today, however, church services have become quite costly. Unless deliberate efforts are made to keep churches open and accessible to all, the lower classes will increasingly be excluded from them. Because there is no widespread agreement on religious doctrine, society has been compelled to leave religious teaching entirely to private initiative. Yet this very fact strengthens the argument for why the State must make other forms of education—particularly secular education—as freely available as possible.

It is now too late to hope that the lower classes will, on their own, discover and adopt a better way to consume wealth. Every step forward in society makes it clearer: more public education must be provided if the weaker parts of the population are to be guided along the same upward path that the more advanced sections have already traveled. Society must either adopt a bold and far-reaching educational strategy—or turn a blind eye as the destructive currents of modern life gradually drag the vulnerable and the unguarded into lives of suffering and moral decay.

www.ingramcontent.com/pod-product-compliance
Lightning Source LLC
LaVergne TN
LVHW100733061126
851857LV00011B/516
* 9 7 8 9 3 7 2 4 4 9 1 8 1 *